THE LITURGY OF ST JOHN

Bishop Lyttelton
Library

Winchester

Gordon S. Wakefield

The Liturgy of
St John

Epworth Press

British Library Cataloguing-in-Publication Data available

7162 0413 4
First published 1985 by
Epworth Press
Room 195, 1 Central Buildings, Westminster, London SW1H 9NR

Typeset by Gloucester Typesetting Services
and printed in Great Britain by
Billing and Sons Ltd, Worcester

Contents

It has sometimes seemed to me that one could compare the structure of the Fourth Gospel to that of a great cathedral. At the entrance is the fine west front and the inner porch, and these correspond to the prologue in 1.1–18 and the secondary prose prologue in the rest of ch. 1. Through the entrance one enters the nave, the place of public worship, supported by its pillars; and this corresponds to the Lord's public ministry of the great signs and discourses, which begins with ch. 2 and is formally closed at the end of ch. 12. Then the building narrows down to the choir, where worship is of a more intimate kind; and to this correspond the discourses of chs. 13–16; for in these the world is shut out, and the Lord reveals the heart of the matter to those who are called 'his own'. Then the building narrows further towards the altar and to what lies beyond the altar. So the Gospel reaches its climax in the passion and resurrection.

Christopher Evans, 'Christ at Prayer in St John's Gospel'

Foreword

This book falls into the category of 'devotional' writing or works on spirituality, and a good deal of it comes from addresses on various occasions, including the Anglo-Catholic Congress at Loughborough during Easter 1983, when I had the honour of being invited to give the Bible studies. In chapter 2 there are echoes of what I said during the weekend of Recollection at Canterbury in April 1984, when the Archbishop invited fifty church leaders to a time of quiet and prayer together. What I said in that context was different in shape and intent from what is found here, and was published both in 'One in Christ' and in a pamphlet which included all those talks, *One in Prayer* (BCC/CTS). But some of the paragraphs are identical. They owe much to some hours spent with Dr G. F. Nuttall.

The study as a whole is an attempt to illustrate a conviction of mine which is not held by most writers on spirituality. I do not believe that when we seek to be led into prayer, communion with God, we should abandon critical scholarship. Bultmann's great commentary on *The Gospel of John* is perhaps more capable of bringing me to prayer than William Temple's *Readings*. I do not accept some of his redaction-criticism and re-arrangements. The union in one man of extreme critic, Lutheran Christian and existentialist philosopher seems to give a bias as obvious as it is unique. But here is a work of devotion and dedication beyond most of our poor attempts to reach God by spiritual techniques. Similarly with Ernst Käsemann's *The Testament of Jesus*. I cannot agree with his thesis. John 17 is a prayer, not in the genre of testaments. Nor do I think it at all correct to speak of John's 'naively docetic'

christology. But though Käsemann may seem to remove the
Gospel ever further from the Jesus of history, and from the
Catholic church, one remains haunted by the sheer power and
wonder of it all and brought close to worship. I accept that this is
because I am a person brought up in the tradition of European
culture which has united, in a Benedictine phrase, 'love of learning and desire for God'. Today we are rightly aware of other
cultures and other forms of Christianity. The word of God has
always spoken from the Bible to the poor and humble who shame
by their insight the learned and the wise. There are groups of
Christians among the Black Churches in Britain, as well as in
Africa and Latin America, where Christian faith is strong, who
know next to nothing of the 'thought-worlds' of the testaments,
who ask no questions born of sophisticated nervelessness and
doubt, but who find a direct summons to faith and sacrifice in the
miracle stories, for whom the longer ending of St Mark's Gospel
comes true. They have support from the latest fashion of literary
criticism far outside the church. ('Structuralism', in so far as I
understand it, abandons concern with original meanings or authors'
intentions but fastens on the text before us *now*.) They have
much to teach us and the communion of faith would seek truth in
a partnership between their naive but prophetic understanding
and the patient asceticism of true scholarship. A Christian group
in Brazil was studying the miracle of the Feeding of the Five
Thousand. In that impoverished country ravaged by unemploy-
ment, they asked 'To what action does this story call us?' They
fastened on the five loaves and two fishes and said 'Let five families
in work look after two families unemployed!' They asked no
questions about what happened or must we expect miracles. A
peripheral detail was the word of God to them. Yet no one can
study the Bible without being in some sense a critic. Jesus himself
was such in his republication of the Jewish law. And there are
stumbling-blocks and inconsistencies to be resolved. What is more,
terrible things have been done by warrant of scripture, atrocities
after the model of Joshua; Cromwell's massacres at Drogheda and
Wexford, ghastly deeds done by Christian sects today, who would
slay their enemies and sing 'Our God reigns'.

I am also of a mind that the age-long harmonization of the Gospels in liturgy and devotion is mistaken, and often conceals from us in a pious haze the piercing lights which shine from each in turn. To harmonize may protect us from certain disturbing questions. In the end it leads to superficial exegesis and an obscuring of the truth.

I have come far since I read Browning's 'A Death in the Desert' for Higher School Certificate in 1938/9, or heard Professor C. H. Dodd's exuberant and inspiring lectures at Cambridge ten years later. I am indebted to Hoskyns, especially, to Barrett, Brown, Lindars and Schnackenburg, as ever to Hort, *The Way, the Truth, the Life,* and to the less well-known W. H. Cadman, *The Open Heaven.* I doubt if the book could have been written without the resources of our magnificent library at The Queen's College, Birmingham. I wish I had discussed it more with my colleagues. The scattered references to the Fourth Gospel throughout the writings of Professor Donald MacKinnon have fed me for years, as has the friendship of Professor Christopher Evans. I cannot think that this will pass the scrutiny of his acute and learned mind should he feel it worth reading. But it owes much to conversations over the years, in which I have been for most part the listener, but which have been for me not only stimuli of friendship, but, in the sense of what I have said above, a 'spiritual' experience.

The book may be criticized because it is neither 'pure' scholarship, nor 'pure' devotion and nods every now and then in the direction of academe while being mostly of the pulpit. But I am trying to bridge the gulf.

The attempt to interpret St John's final chapters in terms of a liturgy may do more than provide a peg on which to hang interpretation. It may shed some light on John's somewhat oblique eucharistic theology, and help Christians to understand better the holy mystery, which is always in danger of being seen in wrong proportion, and yet proclaims the truth as it is in Jesus, and joins his people to his prayer.

Gordon S. Wakefield

Introduction

'He speaks of St John's Gospel with a kind of hushed awe; it is like Fra Angelico, he cannot venture to criticize a verse without a prayer.'[1] So said Henry Scott Holland, an eloquent Anglican canon, of his older contemporary, B. F. Westcott, a renowned commentator on the Fourth Gospel. Many have felt like that, and not only people of learning with Oxbridge connections, or poets such as Wordsworth and Browning, but men and women from all walks of life.

James Barrie's sentimental story *A Window in Thrums* gives an authentic picture of a lowland town when the kirk ruled and the griefs and sorrows of hard-working humble folk were assuaged by the Sabbath sermon and family prayers in the spirit of Burns' 'A Cottars Saturday Night'. Towards the end, the narrator describes the last evening a family were to spend together. One son had been killed years before, as a boy whose heart was already set on being a minister. The younger son is due to return to London by sea, and he and the invalid mother, the daughter, somewhat frail, and the father, not clever, nor fluent, nor well read outside the scriptures, gather around the fire for their customary act of devotion. Hendry, the father, turns over the leaves of his Bible till they come to the place where the book almost falls open anyhow, his favourite chapter, John 14.

Let not your heart be troubled: ye believe in God, believe also in me. In my Father's house are many mansions; if it were not so I would have told you. I go to prepare a place for you.

These words he later takes into his prayer.

It is not difficult to see why the Fourth Gospel and these last discourses in particular have evoked such reverence and such love. They have an other-worldly power which rouses feelings which reach to the emotional depths of one's being. As this Christ speaks every nerve pulsates. Are we not here in closest touch with the very ground of the universe?

Some may demur. Hendry in Thrums and Cambridge scholars last century believed that here we have the very words of Jesus recalled with accuracy over the decades, spoken with divine authority. It is not easy for us so to read St John. There is no reason to think that an aged apostle who had been a companion of Jesus and an eye-witness could not have reproduced with fair exactitude after half a century or more what he had heard. Why cannot we accept the long tradition, reported by Irenaeus of Lyons in the late second century, that John the Son of Zebedee was the beloved disciple, that he lived to a great age in Ephesus and there published his account, fruit of long meditation, of 'the things concerning Jesus'?[2] The dying apostle in Browning's 'A Death in the Desert', a poem which deserves to be taken seriously as an interpretation of the Fourth Gospel, says of the relation between the historic events of Christ's ministry and his book:

> What first were guests as points, I now knew stars,
> And named them in the Gospel I have writ.

The difficulty is that there is no hint from the New Testament, nor in Christian writings of the early second century, that John of the twelve was ever in Ephesus. What is certain is that the Gospel did not find ready acceptance in the church as a whole and Irenaeus was probably fighting for its recognition as the orthodox *fourth gospel*, ready to stand with Matthew, Mark and Luke as authentic and definitive statements of Christian faith over against the many weird and legendary records of Jesus; hence his exposition of the mystic significance of the number four. He may well have confused an elder or presbyter John at Ephesus with the apostle.

The greatest problem is, however, the difference in idiom and in theology from anything else in the New Testament apart from the Johannine letters; the Gospel's indebtedness to sources removed from Palestine and the thought-world in which Jesus lived. In consequence there is an uncertainty born of the study of the Gospel itself in comparison with the others, and of increased knowledge of the religious life and thought of its contemporaries. The conclusion is inescapable that, although St John describes historic events in the life of a historic person, and details of its chronology may be right in some places against that of the synoptists – the length of the ministry for instance and the dating of the Passover – it is more concerned with controversies among the Christians of its own time, than with an historian's record in the modern sense, or a disciple's reminiscences. The Jesus of St John bears a relation to the actual teacher of Galilee and Jerusalem not dissimilar to that of the Socrates of Plato's *Dialogues* to the Athenian philosopher. The comparison must not be forced in other ways. The subject-matter of the Gospel is very different from Plato and so is the dialectic. Here is no disclosure of principles but a life, and its words and deeds decisive for the destiny of us all. But for some people the doubts as to St John being a verbatim report will change the nature of its authority, even if it does not destroy it.

Some find John the least congenial of the evangelists. My own teacher, Robert Newton Flew, relegated the Fourth Gospel to the end of his treatment of the New Testament in his two influential books, *The Idea of Perfection in Christian Theology* and *Jesus and His Church*. There are those who consider the Jesus of St John 'positively repellent', more like a Greek icon than a man of flesh and blood, in spite of his anger and grief. Sometimes his human needs seem to be recorded simply to illustrate the theological mystery of his being. He teaches by sermonic monologue, with such dialogue as there is largely to show the incomprehension and obtuseness of enemies and disciples alike. There are no parables in the synoptic mode, which, though they puzzled his followers as much as the 'figures' or 'riddles' of St John, are vivid stories from nature or human life, and must often have been of topical interest. In the Passion story one misses the 'terror and dismay' of Gethsemane and the cry of dereliction on the cross. Dreadful as they are, they are the very heart of the Gospel, 'recalling our imaginations', as Donald MacKinnon has said 'to a figure prostrate on the earth, afraid and desolate, bidding men and women see in him the ground of all creation'.[3]

Some would level a charge of anti-semitism against John, who calls those who clamour for Christ's death, 'the Jews'. This may have had its share in Christian persecutions of the Jews and in the judgment reversed only by the Second Vatican Council that they were guilty of the hideous crime of deicide. But no author can be blamed for the use that perverts make of his work. The label 'anti-semitic' is an anachronism, a reading back of later tendencies and terms. Nor is it correct, though we must remember that the Christians with whom he was concerned would feel threatened by the power of their Jewish opponents, as well as by surrounding paganism and their own divisions. But John nowhere condemns a whole race. There is no terrible cry as in St Matthew where the people with one voice shout, 'His blood be upon us and on our children.'

(Charles Wesley managed to find in this a *double entendre*

> Each moment applied
> My weakness to hide
> Thy blood be upon me and always abide.

His doing so is Johannine in its irony.) And John is not concerned simply with the screaming mob at the trial of Jesus but with some of those to whom the Gospel is directed. They are 'the Jews', though they may be of Gentile race; and so perhaps are we. But if the enemies of Jesus were a rabble of Jewish nationalists resembling National Front thugs, or those who wreaked slaughter in the Refugee Camps of the Lebanon, or the terrorists of any race, many of his friends were Jews. Nathaniel is 'an Israelite indeed' and Nicodemus assists at the Lord's royal burial. And what of the Mother of Jesus, never called Mary in this Gospel, whom some think represents at the foot of the cross the Jews who had become Christians and according to the evangelist were in the true succession?

Whether John knew the Synoptic Gospels, as used to be pre-supposed, or simply was aware of the tradition about Jesus which they proclaimed in their writings, and which may have existed in John's church in a less pure form, we shall never discover. We could not do without them, though they are not without problems for us today and hardly constitute an easier option, even if they offer a more human, more compassionate Christ. But John's challenge cannot be disregarded. Not only does he force us to ask the liberal theologian's question, 'What must Jesus really have been like if he could be so presented sixty years after?' There is a more searching issue. Hort expressed the claim of the Fourth Gospel 'in the form of two separate doctrines; first, that the whole seeming maze of history in nature and man, the tumultuous movement of the world in progress has running through it one supreme dominating Way; and second, that he who on earth was called Jesus the Nazarene *is* that Way.'[4] Do we believe it?

Browning, to quote him again, put it like this:

> Call Christ, then, the illimitable God
> Or lost.

We may want to qualify that. Jesus for John is not the whole of 'the illimitable God'. There is along with the statement 'I and the Father are one' a certain subordinationism, 'The Father is greater than I'. Jesus is God as he has revealed himself to humanity. He is altogether God. The Nicene faith is a logical development of the Fourth Gospel. Jesus is of one substance or being with the Father. Jesus reveals no secondary Deity but the Most High God. 'Yet', as Barrett goes on to say, 'he is *Deus revelatus*; not the whole abyss of God, but God known.'[5]

Nevertheless this is the question with which St John confronts us, the existential choice we are called upon to make. 'This is life eternal to know thee the only true God and Jesus Christ whom thou hast sent.' Do we believe it?

One of the puzzles of the Fourth Gospel lies in its omissions, or, more precisely, what John includes as well as what he leaves out. Some of the Synoptic stories he tells again, even if with a difference. One thinks immediately of the Feeding of the Five Thousand. Yet there is no transfiguration, no agony in the garden, no institution of the eucharist.

I think there are two reasons why these are not recorded. One, because in some sense, the whole of the Gospel is concerned with each of them; and the whole ministry of Christ as John understands it. 'We beheld his glory' is true of every incident from the marriage at Cana to the lifting up on the cross. Every moment the Son does his Father's will; while the depth and horror which he cannot be spared may be conveyed in the account of the descent into the grave of Lazarus and the deep disturbance of soul he feels in the last days at Jerusalem and in the presence of the traitor; John would understand Pascal's thought that Jesus will be in agony until the end of the world. As for the eucharist, it is in the totality of his life and death that Christ gives the bread which is his flesh for the life of the world.

Secondly, the Johannine church may have been in danger of misunderstanding these events. The transfiguration may have been interpreted as a theophany in denial of incarnation; a god 'has come down in the likeness of men', not 'God made man with man to dwell'. Meditation on the agony may have caused Christians even then to brood on the suffering and broken heart of Christ, rather than to find strength in his serenity and victory in his pain. Here is no 'pitiful' Saviour, and though Jesus may have been physically prostrate beneath the Paschal moon, he is in fact our glorified Head, eternally one with the Father, the crown of thorns no instrument of torture but a declaration of kingship. If we never see beyond his agony, we may remain timid in a theology of despair, doped and inactive in the battles of his love. The liberation theologians and their followers have reacted against the traditional Catholic piety of Latin America because it so often left people hopeless in their oppression as they contemplated the Lord himself nailed and bleeding on the cross. It was somewhat different in mediaeval Europe when to gaze on Christ in agony had homeopathic effect; 'only a suffering God can help'. John holds the sufferer and the victor together. In the reality of obloquy, defeat and death he sees the victory which overcomes the world, and which ordains the friends of the Crucified to suffer and triumph with him.

As for the eucharist, there is no anti-sacramental polemic in

John; but there may have been in the church John knew a tendency to trust in the eucharist and not in Christ, to set greater store by the means than the grace, the sign than the thing signified. And there were many pagan analogues in the religious meals of the ancient world. The Gospel could easily have been turned into a cult.[6] It could be that even then the protest of a George Fox would have been justified.[7] The early Quakers disallowed the ordinances, not because they had some romantic and rather pompous notion that all life is sacramental, but because, as Fox said in conversation with a Jesuit:

> For after ye have eaten in remembrance of his death, then ye must come into his death and die with him if ye will live with him as ye apostles did. And it is a nearer and a further state to be in ye fellowshippe with him in his death than to take bread and wine in remembrance of his death.

At the British Faith and Order Conference at Nottingham in 1964, I was a member of the group to discuss worship. A Quaker lady was saying that she did not need the outward elements of bread and wine to be the instruments of communion with Christ or with his people. She could attend the eucharists of Christians which used this ordinance and was not scandalized because she could not partake. The then Bishop of Ripon, John Moorman's, eyes shone. This was precisely his experience at the Second Vatican Council then in session. Day by day he went and communed spiritually, though 'a separated brother'. He did not feel deprived from the grace of the sacrament, though he longed for the visible unity in the one Body which receiving the sacred species would have signified.

John might have understood; though one cannot be sure because throughout the Gospel he lays such heavy, almost exaggerated emphasis on the physical – 120 gallons of wine at Cana, the man at the pool for 38 years, the man *born* blind, Lazarus four days in the tomb and stinking, the eating and drinking the flesh and blood of the Son of Man. Yet after that last carnality (it is not cannibalism?), Jesus says 'The spirit alone gives life; the flesh is of no avail; the words which I have spoken to you are both spirit and life.'

In the last chapters of St John all is word and deed. The nearest one gets to a ritual act until the breakfast by the lakeside, and that is a meal rather than a liturgy, is the foot-washing. But later he says 'You are clean through the word which I have spoken to you'; on which Augustine comments:

> Jesus does not say 'You are clean because of the baptism with which you have been washed' but 'because of the word which I have spoken unto you'. Take away the word and what is the water but (plain) water? But when the word comes into association with the material element, a sacrament comes into being as though the word itself took visible form – not because the word is spoken but because it is believed.

Augustine may be thinking of the baptismal liturgy and the triple interrogation of candidates in answer to which they professed their faith. But he understands John's sacramental theology, in which the word is paramount.

In our time we are barraged by words and are too punch-drunk to listen, while other media of communication proliferate and may have more influence on the psyche. In his novel *A Passage to India*, published in the 1920s, E. M. Forster has as one of his characters an elderly Englishwoman who had almost fainted in a tour of echoing caves. Resting from her ordeal, she was trying to write a letter but was interrupted by a sense of despair and of her own insignificance in the scheme of things.

> But suddenly at the edge of her mind, Religion appeared, poor little talkative Christianity, and she knew that all its divine words from 'Let there be light' to 'It is finished' only amounted to 'boum'.

Many in our world suspect that such is the case. We are weary of sermons, of the preponderance of the verbal in worship, and we turn to the old spiritual techniques and seek for God in the silence. But some, less religious, are disrespectful of words because they do not like listening, and are unwilling to submit to the discipline of hearing anyone but themselves.

That our words are too many both to God and other people

may be accepted without demur. But not only is articulate and communicative speech a distinguishing mark of humanity over against the beasts, it is one of the supreme ways of showing love. A woman I once counselled because she feared for her marriage complained that when her husband made love to her he never said anything. A gynaecologist in whose hearing I mentioned this told me that this was a frequent factor in marital breakdown. We all know of the false lover, eloquent in his praises and his promises whose devotion is words and nothing more; but the silent, wordless lover may appear as though he wants possession and satisfaction and does not recognize how much the object of his attentions needs the assurance and the dignity that words alone can give.

This brings us very near to the heart of the Fourth Gospel. No one has expounded what the word means to John more cogently than the Göttingen scholar, Ernst Käsemann. 'Jesus' love for his disciples is expressed by his communicating to them the word of the Father (15.15) . . .' This 'is also the essence of the Father's love for the community. Hence, we may infer that the Father's love for the Son from "before the foundations of the world" which, according to 17.24, made him to be the Son and the revealer, can only mean that God has always spoken to Jesus. Therefore he is the exclusive and unique Word of God for the world . . . For John, real communication is impossible without words, discussion, dialogue and, conversely, he understands such dialogue as the communication of one's being and therefore as love.'[8]

In a conversation many years ago with the late Noel Davey, he suggested that we might try to devise a liturgy drawn from St John. If so, the corrollary of the foregoing is that it would be a liturgy of the word. There have been theories that the Gospel is based on a three-year Jewish lectionary cycle, and also that images from the liturgy used in the church to which the author wrote, possibly Ephesus, are frequent.[9] Chapters 14 to 16 read like homilies with some 'discontinuous dialogue', in which the disciples are always 'put down'. It is by no means improbable that John's church, like some students of the Jewish Torah and the Qumran sect, spent long hours in an extended liturgy of the word of which these last discourses are an example. And here is table-fellowship as in the eucharist.

Yet there is more than the Word – or at least more than the words of the Word. The Gospel does not end with Chapter 17, as some would have thought consistent with the evangelist's method and purpose. It goes on to describe what Hoskyns called 'the bloody, concrete event of the Crucifixion', though not in terms which dwell on the torture and indignity. Christ is regal in his shame and sovereign even on the tree. It is almost as though he presides as the celebrant of a great service, though the earthly event is not a rite but a murder. Such glory may be demeaned by a mechanical observance of a too-often repeated ceremony, or by a 'tripping along' to communion; but we may find here a liturgy which is completed not in word alone but in the Word which is Deed.

And there is communion; not only because this is the motif of the discourses, but because as they stand beneath the cross and meet their risen Lord, the disciples receive his Spirit and life and enter into that presence which, to echo Hort, takes its character no longer from their circumstances but from his.

John was writing with the liturgical practice of his church, among other things, in mind, and not uncritically. And it may help to interpret the Fourth Gospel and to allow some of its profundities to surface amid the shallowness of so much of our glib and overconfident understanding, if we expound the last nine chapters like this:

13.1 to 17	The Preparation
13.18 to 38	The Fencing of the Table
14 to 16	The Ministry of the Word
17	The Prayer of Consecration
18 to 20	Crucifixion – Resurrection – Communion
21	Post-Communion.

1 The Preparation

The story of the washing of the disciples' feet has been thought by some to be the fourth evangelist's substitute for the eucharist, an alternative to a sacrament that was already becoming a ritual form rather than a spiritual reality and which needed the corrective of a liturgy less in danger of confusion with magic, or prone to encourage arrogant sacerdotal pretensions. The practice of popes and monarchs washing the feet of beggars on Maundy Thursday, which survives in Britain in the annual distribution by the sovereign of 'Maundy money', without any re-enactment of what Jesus did, may be thought to belie such intention and be as empty a show as the most profane mass. Protestants, however, should be careful about condemning Catholic practices without a very intimate knowledge and some psychological as well as spiritual discernment.

The ancient church associated the foot-washing with the other sacrament, baptism. In some places it was a part of the baptismal office and either preceded or followed the anointing and the vesting with a white robe after the ceremony of baptism. The foot-washing was accompanied by some such words as these:

> I wash thy feet as our Lord Jesus Christ did to his disciples. Thus do thou to guests and strangers. Our Lord Jesus Christ wiped the feet of his disciples with the towel wherewith he was girded. As I do to thee, do thou to strangers, to guests and to the poor.

It was gradually abandoned because of its confusion with baptism. In any case, the Roman liturgy which became dominant in the West had not included it. In the sixteenth century, the

ex-Franciscan, Hinrich Never, preacher at Greyfriars, a Reformer
with Zwinglian ideas on the Lord's Supper and opposed to infant
baptism, held that the true baptism commanded by Christ is the
foot-washing. We cannot ignore the possibility that baptism may
lie somewhere behind the story; if so total immersion is ruled out
as in some early pictures and the design of baptisteries. A similar
instinct has been to see the foot-washing as an act of preparation
for the Lord's Supper, whether in some association with baptism
or not. The Greek Liturgy of the Divine and Sacred Basin may
have originated as early as the fifth century. It has been described
by Hoskyns and Davey as follows:

> The Archbishop, Bishop or Chief Priest, gorgeously vested,
> enters the Church through the great gates of the sanctuary,
> accompanied by twelve priests and the reader of the Gospel
> (the Evangelist). One of the priests takes the part of a door-
> keeper to represent Judas, another of a steward to represent
> Saint Peter. When the choir has sung the introits and appro-
> priate collects have been read, the celebrant, who represents
> Christ, removes his vestments and, girding himself with a towel,
> pours water into a basin and advances to Judas, who rudely
> pushes forward his feet to be washed and kissed, thereby indic-
> ating his hardness of heart. When the feet of the other disciples
> have been washed, the celebrant comes last to Simon Peter,
> who with tears withdraws his feet and shows with his hand, his
> expression and his whole body, his reluctance to be thus washed.
> The dialogue in John xiii is recited, ending with the washing of
> Peter's feet. At the words *Now ye are clean but not all*, the cele-
> brant turns to Judas and points his finger at him. The celebrant
> then returns to his throne, removes the towel and is vested.[1]

One notices how imagination has played on the story and added
details which are not in the scripture. But though we may wish to
remove some of the dramatic as well as the vestimental embroi-
dery, the liturgy sets the foot-washing in its right context as part
of the commemoration of the passion; it 'is dominated by the
thought of the incarnation, the death and the resurrection of the
Son of God'.

A minister of the United Reformed Church known to me often reads the story at the Lord's Supper, very slowly and solemnly, with pauses. Then, after a prayer, he goes on to the words of institution.

The foot-washing and all that it implies is an essential concomitant of the sacrament of Bread and Wine. The eating and drinking may be a mockery without all that this other rite signifies.

The passage deceives us if we think it simple. It is no easier than any other in the Fourth Gospel. Some indeed have thought it a conflation of two accounts. There are certainly two explanations which follow one another in the first seventeen verses of John 13. The first is cleansing through the work of Christ; the second that his disciples should 'follow the example of his great humility'.[2]

The Jewish Passover approaches, though this is no Passover feast, but the ordinary evening meal with the usual blessings and customs (see verse 30), not the solemn commemoration of the deliverance from Egypt. There is no Exodus motif in these chapters. Nor would there be a foot-washing at the Passover.

Jesus is at supper with his disciples, presumably the twelve, though no number is mentioned. Jesus is there as the one who knows; knows that the time of his departure out of this world is at hand; knows that this will be the result of the machinations of human wickedness, brought out into the open by his presence on earth (15.22), and assisted by the treachery of one of his chosen followers; knows, above all, that he is returning to the Father from whom he came. His mission is accomplished.

His heart is filled with love towards those given him by the Father. Not towards all the world. We must think later of the tension between the exclusive and the inclusive in true love. Jesus loves *his own* and loves them 'to the end'. This has a double meaning. He loves them to death (cf. 15.13), and, also, perfectly.

It is in the fullness of his heavenly knowledge and destiny that Jesus leaves his place at table and does the duty of a slave. It is not simply an act of human condescension but of divine disclosure; yet it but lifts a corner of the veil. 'You do not understand now what I am doing but one day you will.' As a dramatic and moving gesture during supper it is a sign which points to what is soon to follow when the divine glory will be revealed in the shame of the cross and the pierced yet unbroken body will be the Bread which is Christ's flesh given for the life of the world.

We must reckon with the variant readings at verse 10. Some manuscripts give a longer version: He who has bathed does not need to wash except for his feet, but is clean all over. This gives an easy explanation and one that is homiletically satisfying, which is perhaps why it was interpolated, if it is not the original. We are cleansed by our entry into Christ of which baptism is the sign, but, like the ancient dinner guest, who has a complete bath before leaving home, yet needs the dust and sweat of the road to be washed from his feet on arrival at his host's, so we must have constant forgiveness of the sins we commit on life's journey. This interpretation was favoured by a Wesleyan Methodist scholar, a superb philologist, James Hope Moulton, in a sermon preached on the story in 1899 '. . . the man whose soul has been purged from the guilt and power of sin moves about among the pollutions of a world of sin, and the defilement cleaves as it were to the feet that tread life's dusty road. He has not returned from the bath to wallowing in the mire; his heart is sound and pure by a living faith in Christ; his sins are not wilful.'[3] Yet such a person has daily to pray 'Forgive me my debts as I also forgive my debtors' and this without any consciousness of apostasy. Moulton argues, with a trace of anti-sacerdotalism, that this washing of grime from the feet, this daily forgiveness, is something the disciples of Jesus are to do for one another. The purpose of this 'neglected sacrament', or, better, acted parable, is *the duty of fellowship among believers for the conquest of daily sin*. This leads him straight to the Methodist class-meeting, where members had to confess their faults to one another, to tell each other of their faults, 'plain and home', but all that they might receive mutual forgiveness. Moulton, at the end of the nineteenth century, is able to recognize that there are those who cannot unburden themselves in a group and need a 'soul-friend', or at most an intimate company of two or three.

Some will recall a poem by the twentieth-century French mystic, Charles Péguy, about the dinner guest needing to get rid of the mud of his walk as he enters the house, but not to go on talking about it which would soil the dining-room.

> To carry so much as the memory and anxiety about mud into
>   the temple
> And then preoccupation and thought of mud
> Is in fact to carry mud into the temple,
> Now mud must not cross the threshold of the door.
> When the guest arrives at his host's let him simply wipe his feet
>   before entering,
> So that he enters clean and with clean feet and then
> He should not always be thinking of his feet and the mud on
>   his feet.
> Well, you are my guests, God says . . .
> You are my guests and my children who come into my temple.
> You are my guests and my children who come into my night.
> On the threshold of my temple, on the threshold of my night,
>   wipe your feet and don't let's mention it again.[4]

This raises the question of the confession of sin before holy communion, and gives justification to the modern custom of a brief, rather perfunctory, corporate confession before the real action of the service begins with the ministry of the word. In the earliest rites, there was no confession, though the worshipper was supposed to enter into the holy celebration free from sin, and, as a neophyte, exorcised. The Protestant reformers were not satisfied with this and placed the confession among the 'table prayers' immediately before communion. 'Sin in believers' was a fact with which they had to live, and they might well have argued that the Christian life is an education into the understanding of our sin as well as a growing liberation from it. Does not the preaching of the gospel show us 'the depth of inbred sin?' And is not the saint the one most conscious of his own imperfections, who even while rejoicing in the triumphs of grace never outgrows the earliest and lowliest of all prayers, 'God be merciful to me a sinner'?

Thus the longer reading has spiritual implications for us to discuss and debate in the light of the development of penitence in church history, and our own experience. The Johannine writings as a whole are important in the church's penitential system. They

seem to point away from rigorism, the severe doctrine of Hebrews
that sin after baptism cannot be forgiven, and yet assert that the
goal of the Christian life is sinless perfection.

> If we say that we have no sin we deceive ourselves and the truth
> is not in us. If we confess our sins, he is faithful and just to forgive
> us our sins and to cleanse us from all unrighteousness (I John 1.8).

> If any man sin, we have an advocate with the Father, Jesus
> Christ the righteous, and he is the propitiation (remedy for the
> defilement) of our sins and not our sins only but the sins of the
> whole world (I John 2.2).

> Sin is lawlessness. And you know that Christ was manifested to
> take away sins and in him is no sin. Whosoever abides in him
> does not sin . . . (I John 3.4–7).

> No one born of God commits sin . . . (I John 3.9).

There is a paradox here, which the epistle resolves by adumbra-
ting the distinction, so prominent in the Catholic moral theology,
between mortal and venial sin. In the terms of the foot-washing
there are sins which may be wiped away as dust on a journey; but
also sins which renounce our very birthright as Christians, indeed
murder the Christ within us, and break our union with God.

The distinction has been useful. And the Fourth Gospel might
give some credence to the Calvinist notion that the elect, Christ's
own, will be kept so safe in the mystical union that they will never
be lost; so they commit only venial sin. The dying Cromwell
asked his chaplain, 'Is it possible to fall from grace?' The chaplain
assured him that it was not. So the Protector died in assurance of
faith, 'for', he said, 'I know I was in grace once.' An evangelical
Anglican rector whom I remember with deep love, once told of a
noted writer of effective books who was an adulterer. The rector
was convinced that his salvation would not be jeopardized but his
reward diminished.

On the other hand, to look ahead to the teaching about the vine
and the branches, some united to Christ are cut off, one must pre-
sume, for all eternity. We dare not be complacent. We must avoid

the extremes of being so sure of God's love that we become indifferent to the sins we still commit as Christians – 'He's a Good Fellow and 'twill all be well' – or so hag-ridden by guilt that we are in total despair, which sometimes leads us further into sin, or gives what Hopkins calls 'carrion-comfort', a feeding on itself which is a form of self-indulgence. Many penitents enjoy their state and therefore will never come to perfect love.

The distinction has been useful. But it is as well not to trust it too closely. So-called venial sins are a sign that we are still to some extent in the grip of evil, and, if tolerated, they may be the roots of worse. We should pray with Charles Wesley:

> O may the least omission pain
> My well-instructed soul
> And drive me to the blood again,
> Which makes the wounded whole.

But if the church of the Johannine letters was not rigorist, we must not necessarily read its practical theology into the Gospel; for the Gospel stands apart from the letters, close as its connection is. It has a greater christological profundity.

With the New English Bible, I prefer the shorter text of John 13.10 'A man who has bathed needs no further washing; he is altogether clean; and you are clean . . .'

The foot-washing is a sign of the cleansing which Christ accomplishes. It is something done for us and to us. Peter did not think that Jesus should wash his feet. He may have been fearful that the hierarchical order in which he was secure was being upset, but in his heart he did not wish to submit to what the Servant-Lord was going to do to him. He was not willing to 'abandon' himself to Christ. He wanted to choose what he thought best for himself, to work out his own salvation, to fulfil his own spiritual ambitions, to sprinkle or immerse himself, or be left dry, according to his will, to withdraw from the circle and be treated differently from the rest. When the Lord so gravely insisted, 'If I do not wash you, you have no part with me', Peter then demanded an excess of ablution: 'not my feet only; wash my hands and head as well.' But Jesus washes his feet and says 'You are clean.' The Son of God did not come down to earth and return again to provide the lustrations of a religion which absorbs us in our own purification. The cross is outside the door of the spiritual bath-house and engages with terrorists and soldiers and demonstrating crowds; it means blood as well as water. But there in Christ we are made clean in spite of the filth and stench and shame of it all.

In Aristotle's *Poetics*, he teaches of *katharsis*, from the same root as the words used in John 13, and of the cleansing effect of tragedy, through the terror and pity which its dramatic representation strikes into our hearts. The death of Jesus, like an ancient or Shakespearian tragedy, has a basis in history, though, as Hoskyns said about the whole of the Gospel, 'it is the non-history that makes sense of the history'. St John releases Christ from time and this world, even though he does so through the 'hour' and for the salvation of the world. Yet Calvary is no Oberammagau. It cleanses us through its actuality, the cosmic change it effects in the relations between God and humanity and the balance of spiritual forces in the universe, not because it may be communicated in an art-form. And Jesus did not command his followers to perform a passion play for his *anamnesis*, but to eat and drink blest bread and wine, and, in John 13, to wash one another's feet. Yet the story of the cross is told in the church's worship and witness, and it is almost tragedy in the classical sense. Much of it may only be understood if we realize how near it comes to the unresolved sorrows and ironies of human life. Reinhold Niebuhr was right. It is 'beyond tragedy'; but not without tragedy. And there is cleansing in the contemplation of the Crucified, as John hints when in 3.15 he compares the lifting up of the Son of Man with the impaling of the brazen serpent in the wilderness; but, for him and those to whom he writes, and all who come after, sight is faith.

But the cleansing seems all connected with John's rather cold and unemotional saying about our having part with Christ – a share in what is to happen to him, to have our lot, our line, our portion in the same place. 'The servant shall be as his Lord.'

A Marcan parallel to John 13 is found in chapter 10 of that Gospel, verses 33ff., where the sons of Zebedee ask to sit one on Jesus' right hand and the other on his left in his glory. They want part with him. And he said to them: 'You know not what you ask. Are you able to drink the cup that I drink, or to be baptized with the baptism that I am baptized with?' It is very suggestive that he refers to a washing with water, though he is talking of his Passion, and he says that they will have part in it, though not in the way they think, so eager are they for their own dignity and precedence. 'The servant shall be as his Lord', though only through the katharsis of having part with him in his death.

This is what it means to be a Christian. To have part with Christ. Not simply to be instructed in the Christian world view, which the English reformers were after when they stipulated that candidates for confirmation should know the Commandments, the Creed and the Lord's Prayer, though they are not to be despised. But to be a Christian is not to have been through a course in Christian education. *It is katharsis not catechesis.* It is to have part with Christ, leading to the union of which the discourses which follow the foot-washing speak, that union with the Father through the Son in the Holy Ghost which is as close as vine and branches, bread and eater, and which is more than a constitutional arrangement, or a business merger.

It is to this union that the great sacraments bear witness and which indeed they convey. James Hope Moulton has a surprisingly intense passage in a communion address:

> With the same absolute conviction with which the savage devours his slain foe in order to take his foe's bravery into himself must the Christian take Christ into every fibre of his being, to penetrate with the Divine might of His self-sacrifice every part of his nature and every energy of his life. Only when we have thus taken Christ into the very depths of our being so that our voice speaks with His tones and our very thoughts are penetrated with his quickening presence, can we be meet instruments in His hand for the salvation of the world He died to redeem.[5]

The consequence of the cleansing which gives part with Christ is that his disciples live with one another in a humility and love corresponding to his own.

'Do you know what I have done to you? You call me Teacher and Lord; and you are right for so I am. If I then your Lord and Teacher, have washed your feet, you ought also to wash one another's feet. For I have given you an example, that you also should do as I have done to you.'

Notice the nature of the Lord's injunction. It is for mutuality. No one in the foot-washing is to take the place of Christ. The eucharist requires a President to perform the actions which Jesus did at table, to repeat the thanksgiving and to make sure that all is done decently and in order; but no such person has place in this act and for pope or sovereign so to imitate Christ is to misunderstand its nature. The Liturgy of the Divine and Sacred Basin, in spite of its theological percipience, leaves one uneasy. 'You ought also to wash one another's feet.' That is the injunction of Christ.

It is fair comment that in ecumenical negotiations too much attention has been given to reconciling hierarchies. Not that questions of authority are unimportant; while the matter of authenticity cannot be brushed aside. How do we know that we have the mind of Christ, that the church as it has developed throughout the ages, in so many mutations influenced by so many cultures, is his body on earth? And order as well as faith cannot be ignored in our ecumenical fellowship, least of all in the confused times in which we live when the whole concept of separated, ordained ministry is being questioned by some of the very elect, while the cult of personality does not diminish in the world and the new breakaway sects and house churches are nearly all dominated by some powerful emergent leader. New presbyter is ever old priest writ larger and larger. Yet it is not just sentimentality which sees the marks of the true church in a life together of self-renouncing love. The hymn Paul quotes in Phil. 2.5–11 is inevitably associated with the foot-washing, though perhaps close examination shows profound differences in understanding of the incarnation: 'Have this mind among yourselves, which you have in Christ Jesus, who, though he was in the form of God, did not count equality with God a thing to be grasped, but emptied himself, taking the form of a servant . . .'

In saying this, we must recognize how clear an understanding

of it there has been in recent times in those communions in which
the historically prejudiced believe it has been most denied. Primacy
is now declared to be a primacy of proclamation, of the uncondi-
tional love of Christ, and of service. Christ's humility may be
more in danger in those churches which claim individual freedom –
as in the house churches already referred to – than in churches of
Catholic order. 'Mitred locks' are not the inevitable accompani-
ments of prelacy. But those words of Christ must never be disregarded: 'If I then your Lord and Teacher have washed your feet,
you ought also to wash one another's feet.' Sacraments will cease
in the kingdom of God, but not this.

A Methodist minister of fifty years since once described a dream
he had had. He thought he was a tourist in heaven and wandered
into the museum of that Holy City. 'There was some old armour
there, much bruised with battle. Many things were conspicuous
by their absence. I saw nothing of Alexander's nor of Napoleon's.
There was no Pope's ring, nor even the inkpot that Luther is said
to have thrown at the devil, nor Wesley's seal and keys, nor the
first Minutes of Conference, nor the last . . . I saw a widow's mite
and the feather of a little bird. I saw some swaddling clothes, a
hammer and three nails, and a few thorns. I saw a bit of a fishing
net and the broken oar of a boat. I saw a sponge that had once
been dipped in vinegar, and a small piece of silver . . . Whilst I
was turning over a common drinking cup which had a very
honourable place, I whispered to the attendant, "Have you not
got a towel and basin among your collection?" "No", he said,
"not here; you see, they are in constant use." '[6]

Jesus washes his disciples' feet and bids them wash one another's.
Do they wash his? Not in the Johannine understanding of him
where he is always Master and Lord and in spite of the intimacy
of the union which he promises and the friendship which he offers,
he remains at a certain distance and is never more regal than when
most humiliated. His feet are anointed by Mary at Bethany, but
not washed. In St Luke's Gospel it is different, and his feet are
washed not in the fellowship of his disciples but when he is a rich
man's guest, and not by Peter and James and John nor any of the
others but by a woman from Soho, we may say, a forgiven sinner

of a public and notorious kind. She cannot restrain her devotion. She washes his feet with her tears.

Käsemann maintains that Zinzendorf's confession also holds true for John. 'I have but one passion. That is he and only he.'[7] The Fourth Gospel both reveals and has inspired a devotion as ardent as the woman's. But Jesus is here the sinless, unblemished Lamb of God on his way to his glory with the Father. He is beyond our sense perception, though his own are forever in his presence. We ourselves, mutually forgiven and humble in love, enter through the cleansing he alone can give into the community which now waits on his word.

2 The Fencing of the Table
John 13.18–33

Before Jesus can speak his words to his own, the traitor must depart. 'You are not all clean', and the one of whom the Devil has taken complete possession must go. There can be no fellowship in the things of God if there is a hostile presence.

Anyone charged with leading worship, or indeed a sensitive participant, can tell if there is that in the midst which mars the peace. One hears these days of some who will interrupt a preacher or a service if they do not think the doctrine 'sound'. Mute opposition, or a spirit of division or enmity unexpressed, except in a poisoned atmosphere, may be worse. It was not unknown in the early church. The other writings of the New Testament do not allow us to accept in its entirety the idealized accounts of *The Acts of the Apostles*. No more then than now were the followers of Jesus 'all with one accord'.

Not all, please God, are Judases. In some ways he is unique; certainly in the Synoptic Gospels. John may feel that there are traitors in his own church, those who will sell Christians for silver. He distinguishes between Judas and Peter, the latter frail, over-bold as he protests too much and shouts down his own weakness; yet he remains within the circle, and, after defection, will be restored. To deny any knowledge of Christ out of fear is cowardly and disloyal and hurtful to the Lord. It is not to conspire his death, to plan to remove him out of this world altogether.

Peter must go on his way, which in these next hours will not be to follow Christ, in spite of his rash declaration. He has not at present the strength of will which endures to the end. But he remains within the group of disciples; and is not ultimately cast out. And he did not mar the fellowship because his heart was with Christ and he wanted to love him. He might be prone to jealousy of the beloved disciple even after the Resurrection, but he was not totally disruptive, nor traitorous.

Judas is different; different from those who break the peace in congregations today as they always have done. They may go far to make life impossible for those who do not share their views, they sin against love and lack magnanimity. Perhaps separation is the only practical answer, though one would hope that they might be brought to reconciliation, not by recanting their beliefs but learning to see that Christ calls others beside themselves. The Way fulfils himself in many ways.

Judas is different. What was the nature of his treachery? There are mysteries about him which St John does not resolve.

It is not easy for us to see him as a 'personality'. He is the treasurer of the group and it is alleged that he was a thief as well as a traitor (12.6). This may be due to a tendency to regard him as evil through and through, but though his whole self is polluted by his treachery, he may have been a good treasurer. Where he stands as a warning even before his dastardly act is in his taxing the woman, and by implication, Jesus, with vain expense. 'Why was not this ointment sold . . . and given to the poor?' The explanation is that he wanted the proceeds not for the poor but for himself, which could be a trifle simplistic. There is a danger that in our desire to use Christian resources in what we believe to be the spirit of the gospel and of Christ's proclamation to the poor and judgment of the rich, we may be exploiting the poor to further our own ends in the church, using them to make the church feel guilty rather than because we are moved by compassionate indignation on their behalf. We may be less than disinterested. Or if we begin with desire for justice and mercy we may in the end become embroiled in policies and actions which do more harm to the poor in their own supposed cause than to any other social class.

But Judas serves a dark purpose. He is held responsible for his deed, and yet it seems as though he is an actor, chosen to play a role in a cosmic drama. He has made his own choice, yet it is all inevitable and foreordained, 'that the scripture might be fulfilled'.

There is here an awareness of the realities of human life and history, however difficult they are for a doctrine of God. 'He who eats bread with me has turned against me.' This, an infringement of all the Eastern laws of hospitality, was the nadir of deception and enmity, yet it happened not infrequently. 'A man's foes are those of his own household.' Human love and friendship have their dark side and sometimes by their very intensity turn to hatred. They have within them the possibilities of hurt and bitterness far worse than that inflicted by obvious and expected foes, whose opposition may be impersonal, and who in any case will not have entered into our hearts, and shared in our disclosures of ourselves. 'Save me from my friends' is a prayer sometimes and tragically justified, not only by their well-intentioned blunders on our behalf, but by the hatred which is so closely related to human love and makes a *new* commandment necessary. Judas must go.

It is astonishing that the disciples are unaware that there is a traitor among them and do not know his identity. This ignorance and doubt is in the Marcan tradition too, where, bemused and frightened, the disciples say to Jesus one by one, 'Is it I?' In St John, they look around, nervous and uncomprehending, and Peter asks the beloved disciple to enquire of the Lord of whom he is speaking.

The disciple 'whom Jesus loved' is impossible to name. He enters the Gospel first at this point and must be thought of as the ideal of discipleship, the one who has close and intimate understanding, who is in the bosom of Christ, as Christ is in the bosom of the Father (1.18), who has the spiritual perception that all disciples should seek. Peter beckons him to say who the traitor is but even he does not know without asking Jesus.

Is it not true that because of our imperfect knowledge of God we do not know evil either? And we cannot trust ourselves not to be its worst exponents. In the midst of moral ambiguities, aware of the turmoil within us, hag-ridden by guilt yet unsure if it is justified and always ready to make excuses when either other people or our own consciences accuse us, we cannot discern between good and evil, and therefore are full of self-doubt.

We in part our weakness know
And in part discern our foe.

And in the church itself, we are not certain where treachery lies. In the early church, the Judases were those who reported Christians to the state, those with inside knowledge, members of the Christian community who sold their fellows for gain. Today we often lack the moral insight which recognizes what or who is going to betray Christ. Is it a matter of behaviour, or of doctrine? Are certain sins unforgiveable; or certain views and interpretations of Christianity destructive of the truth and the product not of ignorance or dim-wittedness but of spiritual evil?

We must take to heart the advice of the writer of the first letter of John: 'Test the spirits to see whether they are from God' (I John 4.1). We need the moral courage in the church to tell people where we believe that, in Christ's name, they are mistaken. And yet to do it as disciples, learners in Christ's school, open to the new truth that God may have to teach us from what we may feel is error. Are we condemning heresy with the purity of Christ, or reacting with the anger and suspicion born of fear that we may be wrong, that our protective convictions may be undermined? Or is it in reality our own sins we see in others, and if they are to be cast out, so should we?

Only Jesus knows who the real traitor is. And he does not so much dismiss Judas or excommunicate him, as expose him to himself and let events take their course, in words echoed centuries later when Lady Macbeth says of the murder she plans, 'If it were done when 'tis done, 'twere well it were done quickly.' Jesus does not expostulate, or plead with Judas, trying to dissuade him. He expects his treachery as inevitable, the action of the father of lies, the enemy of all good. He is relieved when Judas receives the sop and goes out, out into the full light of the Paschal moon, yet into the darkness of the kingdom of evil. 'And it was night.'

The lesson in all this for church discipline is not to undertake heresy or witch hunts; rather to wait until those inimical to the church's life are exposed and withdraw because they must. At the same time, the Fourth Gospel is sharply opposed to sentimentality,

to the naive yet prevelant belief that if we show goodwill, tolerance and friendliness, even the worst and most recalcitrant are
bound to be won over. I am not sure that love, as John understands
it, could extend to enemies, or to 'the world', though here is a
notorious ambivalence. The first letter tells believers plainly, 'Love
not the world'; yet John 3.16 says that God loved it so much that
he gave his unique Son for its salvation, or, at least, to make it
possible for those who believe to have eternal life. But Christian
truth always walks along tight-ropes. And John would say, 'Yes
you must love your enemies, you must love the world, but do
not let this love be such that you are won over by them. Christian
love is always able to detach itself from evil. And it is realistic
enough to know that our enemies may remain our enemies even
though we do try to show them love. Judas will always go out
into the night.'

The church must not be so welcoming to sinners that it con-
dones sin, or blurs the distinction between light and darkness, and
itself betrays truth. And it was not a misunderstanding of the Son
of Man, who in the synoptic traditions receives sinners and eats
with them, which made the eucharist a means of discipline and
would deplore the sentimentality, as well as the departure from
the great tradition, of the 'open invitation' to communion. 'All
who love the Lord may come.' That is a piece of twentieth-
century slackness not supported even in the Methodism of former
days. Of course, Jesus receives sinners and the blessed sacrament
is for those who come in their need and penitence, as battered
pilgrims; but they must be those who are seriously intent on 'the
new life', who want to be delivered from sin and to press on to
perfection. Above all, they should be willing to be reconciled
with those in the fellowship of believers from whom in any way
they are estranged. There should be no sense of rancour or division
as an assembly of Christ's people moves towards his altar.

Jesus has been deeply troubled and heavy with sorrow while
Judas remains. He does not rejoice in his departure, for terrible
events will ensue, and Judas is the only one of the twelve whom
he has lost. But this was inevitable in the conflict between light
and darkness, though none the less tragic; and now that the traitor

has gone and there is no more waiting, Jesus is able to speak as though the glorification of the Son of Man were already complete; and everything to be achieved in his outwardly ignominious and painful departure from this world already accomplished.[1]

The word 'glory' is as dazzling as what it describes, and we may be easily blinded by it as by the direct rays of the sun, so that we reel in confusion and clarity of thought and definition is lost. Without a lengthy etymological excursus which would take us into Hebrew and Latin as well as Greek, three aspects of meaning may be singled out. From its background in the Old Testament, 'glory' denotes the very being or life of God, the divine splendour.

> His glories shine with beams so bright
> No mortal eye can bear the sight.

Yet 'glory' implies that in this divine life, this heavenly mode of existence, other beings, angels and men, may share.

There is also the sense of 'renown'. This is often due to the performance of superhuman deeds and expresses the desire and the need of men and women for self-transcendence. 'La Gloire' in French history often meant extravagance and waste in war, the exploitation of ordinary citizens, the maiming of the 'other ranks', and all for an intangible splendour, the 'bubble reputation', but the shining bubble. It is this which has often driven people on to massive heroism. We cannot believe that we were not made for self-transcendence; 'getting and spending' is not our destiny.

Thirdly there is the idea of 'recognition'. Glory is to be seen, acknowledged, honoured, ascribed. It implies worship. The name of the Eastern Church, 'Holy *Orthodox*', means not correct doctrine, but 'right glory'; and the liturgy is therefore the life of the church and its essential action. 'Glory be to God on high.'

It is strange that Jesus should suddenly declare, 'Now is the Son of Man glorified', because his glory has been manifested throughout his ministry. It is by no means certain that we are justified in paraphrasing the declaration, 'The Word was made flesh,' with Wesley's words, 'He laid his glory by.' That may be appropriate to Phil. 2.5–11, the kenosis passage, but not to John who goes on to say, 'We beheld his glory.' In Jesus is the divine life revealed and recognized by faith. C. H. Dodd said that the incarnation was a 'projection' of the glory of the pre-existence of the Son of God into the life of Jesus the Son of Man. Now as his hour approaches, is indeed at hand, he is returning, freed from limitations and lowliness, into the glory which was his with the Father before the world began. The glory of the Eternal Son, the glory of the Incarnate Word cannot be added to or increased in one sense. Yet the being of God does shine even more brightly to those with the gift of faith because the Son's mission is accomplished, because of a deed which is decisive in the history of the universe.

And if we look ahead to chapter 17, Jesus says there that the glory which the Father has given him, he has given to his disciples. This has been called 'a still fuller, a complete and final glorification'. He is to carry the disciples with him into his heavenly glory. Not at the very moment – 'as I told the Jews, I tell you now, where I am going you cannot come' (verse 33). To make it possible for them to enter into his glory is one of the purposes of his death. It is his return to the Father, it is, if one dare say so, his great and final achievement so to reveal the glory of God as to 'draw all men unto myself' (12.32). But it is also to prepare a place for his disciples, so that he will come again and take them to himself (14.3). They are not ready for this as he speaks. For him the Passion is the way to the resumption of his state with the Father. He has to leave this world, but why by a cross? To be a magnet for all, but to make possible, even though not 'at a clap' the perfecting of his disciples through 'crucifixion-resurrection'.

He gives them meanwhile what he describes as 'a new commandment'. It is something of a *non sequitur* at this point and seems to be an interpolation; yet it fits in so well. They are anxious at the prospect of losing Jesus. Are they who have followed thus far, though with imperfect understanding and congenital frailty, to be in no better case than the Jews, who have rejected Jesus? The answer is well given in the words of Bultmann:

The future is subjected to an imperative! Their anxiety was centred on their own actual existence, but now they are directed towards an existence which has the character of an 'ought'. The illusion that they possess him in such a way that he is at their disposal is confronted by another kind of possession: one that consists in fulfilling a command.[2]

'I give you a new commandment: love one another; as I have loved you, so you are to love one another.'

It is worth remarking that the Protestant Reformers interposed the Ten Commandments at the beginning of the Lord's Supper, possibly to provide an Old Testament lesson. But they chose the summary of the old law, still binding on Christians, to remind them of commandments which were not abrogated and which Christ republished with a yet more devastating fulfilment.

It has, this century, been the custom to offer as an alternative 'the commandments of the Lord Jesus', 'our Lord's summary of the Law' to which the Methodist *Book of Offices* of 1936 added this from John. Such harmonization may not have been altogether appropriate, since this may well replace for the fourth evangelist the second commandment: 'Thou shalt love thy neighbour as thyself.'

The 'new' commandment is at once more exclusive and more overwhelming. Love is confined to the little company of the true Christians, weak as they are. Johannine Christianity has something of the ghetto about it and one sees the force of Käsemann's suggestion that the Gospel may have come, not from the Catholic Church but from a Christian sect, somewhat pietist. But there is an element of pietism in Christianity, not only passionate love of Christ, and life-transforming experience, but an imperative mood of obedience and mutual love within small groups. A learned Jesuit known to me was brought up as a Congregationalist. He does not believe that he renounced his Congregationalism by becoming a Catholic. He feels that this form of the church is totally Catholic and that each discrete company of Christians should partake of the fullness of Catholicity – in communion with the great church, but with its marks reproduced in the local, close-knit body of believers, and there visible, even if in some way separate from the world.

Here again is the tight-rope. John does not use the term 'church'.

Here is no word for ecclesiastics except to number them with Annas and Caiaphas. Yet it is mistaken to write off his Christianity as individualistic, or ghetto-like. He balances delicately between the alternative dangers of introverted sectarianism and a too diffused and remote Catholicity. But is it not true to say that God only can love the world? If we try to, we shall either be sucked into its destructive vortex or lost in happy benevolence. For us love must be particular, or else it is just nice feeling rather than a costly dedication of the whole personality. Is not the real test of love for Christians to live in charity, forgiveness and magnanimity with those who also belong to Christ? We may find our neigh-bours so much more attractive, but that may be because we are not in fact so involved with them as with those who are our fellow-disciples of Christ. These are, some of them, very different from ourselves and not altogether congenial. We may want to argue with them because we seriously differ. We may be jealous of their gifts and seeming success in the church. But here our love has a chance to be real because it is tried and tested and our relations may not be always a superficial politeness and an avoidance of spiritual conflict in social camararderie.

As we have observed, love in St John is closely connected with the word, with speech, communication, self-giving. And this command, 'as I have loved you, so are you to love one another' is in contrast, though perhaps in complement to love of neighbour as oneself. To love oneself is not necessarily the root of all evil. Hatred of others may well be due to hatred of oneself. And the capacity to identify, to be compassionate to others as though you suffered with them is to be Christ-like. Yet it may make our most generous love self-indulgent and perhaps leave us insufficiently detached to do real good. We may wish to make our neighbour dependent on us for our satisfaction rather than his benefit. To love as Christ loves according to St John is to be the exegete of the love of God, to communicate his divine love, besides which our own is so fallible, and to help him to bring others with us into his glory. In these terms it is true that to love somebody is to say 'You will never die.'[3]

Why does Jesus call this 'a *new* commandment'? Because he

transforms the nature of love. But there may be echo here of the words of Jeremiah (31.31) and of the charter-story of the eucharist: 'This cup is the *new* covenant in my blood' (I Cor. 11.25 cf. Mark 14.24). If so, the commandment is not so new; it is of the tradition of those in Israel who had understood before Christ the nature of God and his dealings with our race. But Christian faith would maintain that such understanding was not possible without the work of Christ, that those who knew God and loved him and beheld his glory in previous ages did so because of the retroactive grace perfectly revealed in the incarnation, death and resurrection of the Word made flesh.

3 The Ministry of the Word
John 14, 15, 16

The first word of Christ's preaching to his own is of assurance and comfort. Here is no prophetic challenge, no wish to make them more uneasy than they are. There has been an imperative, though gently uttered. Here is

> . . . the comfort of Christ
> When he spake tenderly
> To his sorrowful flock.[1]

Neither the first disciples around the table nor the Christians of the Johannine church needed to be nagged. The Lord himself, though he has been disturbed and agitated, is now serene, and would impart his own peace of union with the Father to his disciples.

> Let not your heart be troubled; you believe in God;
> believe also in me.

Jesus is going away. The disciples do not know how – so it would seem – but they do not want to lose 'the fellowship of sight and hand' – and voice.

The departure of Christ has recurred often in church history since the crucifixion. Hort, in the nineteenth-century, was not only diagnosing his own time, but looking ahead to the succeeding and terrible century, when he wrote:

The eve of the Passion is not the only time when Christ has seemed to His Church to be departing from the earth of which for a while he had been a denizen, and when those whose course has been in great part shaped by the discipleship to Christ which surrounded them have felt with dismay that sustaining habitudes were passing away. His own palpable presence in the flesh has its counterpart, at least as regards the sense of security which it afforded, in a 'Christian world', an assemblage of nations where deference to His Name and acquiescence in His authority receive full public and private recognition. When it becomes manifest that a Christian world in this sense is ceasing to exist, either because Christ's authority is becoming limited to a single narrow department of individual life, or because His right to authority is being questioned altogether at its fountain-head, then the band of His disciples may naturally feel as though He were once more leaving them to themselves.[2]

Those of us who have lived for more than half-a-century in which, not so much through holocaust as through secularization, Christian hopes in the Western world have been belied and the churches have steadily diminished in influence and strength, may well ask not 'Where is the promise of his coming?', but 'Is he not leaving us for good?' There is hope in Africa where more people become Christians in a week than in a year in France, and in Latin America where the churches have revived in the struggle against oppression. For these we thank God and from them we must learn. But it is not likely that missionaries from Africa, though they may revive churches in some places, would re-convert Europe from its post-Christian disillusion. Nor is it clear that African Christianity will remain unscathed by technology and the difficulties of a religious world-view in a universe penetrated by the gadgets of science. And although we may speak of God's judgment on Europe and think that we have brought about our own ruin by iniquities all over the globe, often in the name of Christ, it is by no means certain that an objective analysis would demonstrate that we have been responsible for a greater measure of cruelty or proportion of evil over good than any other civilization, past, present or to come. And no Christian victim of European exploitation or English snobbery should rejoice if the saving remembrance of Christ's love is obliterated from our common life.

To us, penitent for the crimes and failures of our ancestors in the faith, and fearful that we may be losing him forever, not only through the decline of our Christian culture, but in the revival, here and there, of forms of faith which seem lacking in the full amplitude of truth, the Johannine Christ speaks to us as to his own long ago.

But he makes a demand: 'Believe in God, believe also in me.' And he makes an absolute and, for many today, scandalous claim: 'I am the way, the truth and the life; no one comes to the Father but by me.'

That is where assurance starts. And many Christians find it hard to accept. They have become more aware, through immigration, and broader education, of other faiths. In many of our most densely populated places, it is simply not true to say that Christianity deserves greater civic and social privileges than other religions. The hegemony of Anglican establishment could well be abolished, not through the recognition as equal partners of other Christian churches, but through the fact that Christians are no longer proper representatives of what people believe and practice. And once fear and suspicion are cast out and 'dialogue' with other faiths starts, as it should, Christians begin to perceive that they have a monopoly neither of truth, nor of virtue. It has long been questioned by some whether we ought to try to convert Jews; many would feel doubts about attempts to evangelize Muslims or Hindus, though this may disturb some black Christians. The uncertainty grows because so often we talk to the finest and most saintly adherents of other faiths, and contrast them, to our humiliation, with compromised, quarrelsome, intolerant Christians.

How can we accept that Jesus is the only way to the Father? Nineteen hundred years of history and our own increasing experience make us want to say, unless we are fundamentalists as unpleasant as the disciples of the Ayatollah Khomeini, that God fulfills himself in many ways, and Jesus may be one, but only one.

But make no mistake; the claim of the gospel is unequivocal. 'I am the way, the truth and the life; no one comes to the Father but by me.'

It is true that if these words are related to the Fourth Gospel as a

whole, there is greater comprehensiveness. The human Jesus is the
manifestation of the Eternal Word, the real light that enlightens
every man. To Pilate, Jesus will say, 'Everyone who is of the truth
hears my voice' (18.37), while, earlier, he has declared that all who
are in the tombs will hear the voice of the Son of Man 'and come
forth, those who have done good to the resurrection of life, and
those who have done evil to the resurrection of judgment' (5.28, 9).
We could deduce from all this that Jesus is decisive for all human
history and that men and women of other faiths and the saints of
the past, in so far as they hear and obey the truth, are in the fellowship of those who come to the Father, through him and his word,
though they have not consciously known and served him. All
unawares they have travelled by that way, which in Christian
understanding is the Person of Christ. Karl Rahner has talked of
'anonymous Christians'.[3]

The difficulty is that while this possibility of Johannine comprehensiveness may satisfy Christians who have come to respect other
faiths, admire their good and wish for unity with them, this way of
thinking and speaking does not always commend itself to non-
Christians. Though benign and well-intentioned it is felt to be a
form of imperialism, in that it asserts the final truth of Christianity.
To be told that they are Christians without knowing it does not
please them. They may recognize the right of Christianity to exist
and reciprocate by seeing much good in it. But they do not want
to be Christians. Insistence that they are so anonymously is both
uncomplimentary and patronizing.

Perhaps we should, with W. F. Howard, find a solution in the
thought that Jesus says, 'No one comes to the *Father* but by me.'
'The uniqueness of the revelation in Christ is that in him we have
the Way to the *Father*. By the secret of his perfect filial consciousness he brings us through his renewing Spirit into fellowship with
the Father.'[4]

There is that in Christianity which is distinctive and which
meets a human need, which may not be so decisively answered in
the fundamental assertions of other faiths, but to which they have,
in process of evolution, come to supply so that there may be a
similarity to the gospel in their developed forms which was not

there in the beginning. The idea of the Fatherhood of God may be an example, especially as it is seen in the Lucan parable of the Prodigal Son, where there is a divine initiative to meet the returning sinner. The father has been waiting and watching for his son's return all the long years of his alienation and abuse of freedom. In St John there is nothing so conspicuously 'evangelical', in that Jesus is not portrayed as 'the friend of publicans and sinners'; but he is the good shepherd, he has sheep which are not of the narrow fold of Judaism, and, above all, the Father's love is outgoing. The Word is spoken. The Son, 'of the Father's heart begotten', is given for love of an evil world. There is in John a constant divine outpouring from the water become an almost unlimited quantity of wine at Cana to the 'living' water which flows from Jesus and from the Spirit-filled believer (7.37), and the blood and the water from the pierced side of the body on the cross. This is the truth which Christianity exists to proclaim and which it must never surrender in any concordat with other religions.

Bultmann writes – in connection with the sayings about the Good Shepherd in John 10 – of 'the intolerance of the revelation'. And perhaps he supplies the answer to the problem.

He submits that in their quest for reality men must always be tolerant of one another. Where it is a matter of human initiative, where we are honest seekers after truth, we must respect one another's integrity, even if we cannot accept one another's discoveries. But the revelation demands 'absolute recognition'.

. . . the believer does not commit himself to the revelation in order to champion its cause, but only in order to listen to it, to recognize its victory. His intolerance is not a denial of the sincerity and seriousness of the non-believer's commitment. For in this respect the non-believer may often be both a model and a reproach to him. As a man he must tolerate his fellow. His intolerance consists in refusing to make concessions in gaining a hearing for the revelation, for the claim of that power which has made all human commitment obsolete and illusory. It consists in upholding the 'truth' that all human commitment and endeavour, through which man seeks to find his true being, is doomed to fail; that the revelation demands that man abandon his attempt to find himself by giving himself up to this or that cause, because God in his revelation has already given himself up for men; that Jesus has come to give life and fullness.[5]

This leads us to ask whether the real answer to the problem of Johannine exclusiveness may not be found in the vehement protest of the early Karl Barth that Christianity is not a religion.[6] It may have become one through the process of the centuries through inevitable accommodations with the world and the need for it to be stabilized and grounded in institutions. But if these seek to guard the revelation they may also destroy it and turn the gospel into something which it never truly was – one more system by which people try to save themselves through an elaborate apparatus of rites and rules.

Early Christianity appeared to its contemporaries to be irreligious and was charged with atheism because it had no public piety and Christians did not participate in sacrifice. It did not enter the world as a new religion. Perhaps this is why in the Acts of the Apostles, it was called 'the Way' (Acts 9.2), and this may lie behind John's use of that term in Chapter 14. And may not John's uncertain attitude to the sacraments be due to his fears that in the Gentile world Christianity was becoming a cult, just as Paul dreaded that it become another law?

Paul and John did not win, though the Reformation of the sixteenth century and the Vatican Council of the twentieth were very much influenced by a rediscovery of the former. John's place in the Reformation may be yet to come; there may be glimpses of his understanding in certain aspects of Quakerism, though not in some of its christological vagueness and lack of positivism, nor in the excesses of its early 'enthusiasm'. We cannot now abandon our Christian constitutions and our shrines, which have enriched human life as well as at times imprisoned the Spirit and made us too subservient to the religious urges of the human race rather than to the Way, which is Christ. What we dare not do is sanctify our institutions and our orders as though they were divine, whereas they are partial and provisional, signs more of religiosity than of the Word, even though they have often been hallowed by what has been thought to be a doctrine of the incarnation.

Jesus Christ is 'the way, the truth and the life'; not a system of carefully formulated beliefs, nor orders of worship, nor canon law, nor mystical techniques, nor political programmes, nor moral precepts, nor religious experience. He is a person and in union with him, we are led to the Father, who loves us and seeks us in the Son. It has been suggested that the text be translated with the same idiom as Hebrews 10.19ff., 'I am the true and living way', but this does not do justice to it. Jesus *is* the truth. Again we turn to Bultmann:

> One does not come to him to ask about truth; one comes to him as the truth. This truth does not exist as a doctrine, which could be understood, preserved and handed on, so that the teacher is discharged and surpassed. Rather the position a man takes vis-à-vis the Revealer decides not whether he *knows* the truth, but whether he *is* 'of the truth', that is whether his existence is determined by the truth, whether the truth is the ground on which his existence is based.[7]

Bultmann goes on to say that 'in Christianity everyone has to start for himself from the beginning ... each generation has the same original relation to the revelation'. He denies that there is such a thing as 'a history of Christianity within world history, in the sense of a history of ideas, in which one progresses from stage to stage, from solution to solution'. So much for the idea of development and 'the holy tradition'!

Bultmann is right in what he affirms about the Johannine belief that we are in every generation as near to Christ as were those around the table, and that we have to make a decision for ourselves, apart entirely from what we have been told about Christianity, or the record of its past. Perhaps the 'ego eimi', the I AM replaces any command to perform a rite 'in *remembrance* of me'. Where we may disagree is that Bultmann ignores the profound truth in the concept of 'the historic Christ in his fulfilment'. 'Have I been so long time with you and have you not know me, Philip?' The Lord's words are reproachful, but Hort saw them as 'the language

in which we may still hear our Lord recalling us to an undervalued
and imperfectly used experience'.

> ... the Church has for its guidance a fresh accession of know-
> ledge of the Way, not shared by the original disciples. It poss-
> esses its own experience as they possessed and bequeathed theirs.
> The history of the Church from its foundation to the present
> hour is hardly less necessary to the Church at large than the
> Gospel itself, whatever it may be to the individual disciple. For
> the Church now to enquire concerning a Way for itself, with-
> out study of the Way as revealed in its own history, would be
> as though the apostles had stripped themselves of the memories
> of what they had heard and seen and looked upon and handled
> by way of preparation for going forth among the nations.[8]

This history is not all of failure and perversion – a somewhat
mixed chapter in a history of world religions. And the real tradition is of love and prayer, through living voices, which speak
from 'communion with the heart of the faith', and have 'immediacy and directness' which incarnate encounter with the Lord.
Christian liturgy is not simply the rubrics of decency and order;
it is the record library of these living voices, as is the fellowship of
'soul-friends'. We may speak, even if the phrase be inelegant, of
'mediated immediacy'.

Jesus is the life. 'I am come that they might have life and might
have it to the full' (10.10). 'I am the Resurrection and the life'
(11.25), the more so since he, who was such from the beginning,
has passed through mortal death. Through him we are not at the
mercy of the boredom, frustration and sufferings of the road that
is 'a gloomy merging' into nothingness; we share the very life of
God.

'Believe in God, believe also in me.' 'I am the way, the truth
and the life.' That is where comfort begins in a world which Jesus
seems to be leaving. But because he goes to the Father there are
benefits in his absence greater than in his presence. 'It is expedient
for you that I go away.' Let us consider them.

First, his disciples have a habitation in the Father's house. 'In my
Father's house are many mansions; if it were not so I would have

told you; for I go to prepare a place for you.' This promises believers a home in the eternal order, secure beyond the ravages of time and death. It also enlarges their horizons and sets them in a larger universe than that between the cradle and the grave. Already they claim their inheritance in the life of the world to come, but this is not simply the hope of a personal reward after death, a dwelling place in some heaven of our worldly and fleshly conceiving, which would make life here a self-indulgent dream. It means that earthly existence is seen in the perspective of eternal life, that the new world is called in to redress the balance of the old. This may not only help endurance – this suffering, this seeming desertion by Christ is but for 'a little while' and only part of the infinite progress of the soul – it creates a 'divine discontent' with the conditions of this world both for ourselves and other people, which though it may, as with St Paul, make us long to depart and be with Christ, which is far better, also keeps us, like him, on earth for the sake of the continuing mission to make eternal life available here and now.

But the Lord's absence to gain heaven for us also promises his return. 'I shall come again and receive you to myself, so that where I am you may be also.' This is very different from the apocalyptic expectation of his coming. Here is no advent on the clouds at the crisis of the end of the age. Here are no thunder and lightning, no trumpet to wake the dead, no shaking of the earth's foundations. John does not really make up his mind whether Jesus has returned in the resurrection, or whether we await an end to human history. The matter may not concern him too greatly. The decisive event is the revelation of God in Christ, the judgment has already taken place in his trial hour, the world rolls on in opposition to God, but the succession of obedient believers is safe and sure and full of joy in the life he brings. There is no need to ask, 'Where is the promise of his coming?' It is enough that the promise has been made. In some sense the promise *is* his coming.

The world, of course, is not aware. The last it saw of Jesus was when his body was taken down from the cross and buried in the tomb. The other Judas is puzzled by this and asks, 'Lord what can have happened, that you mean to disclose yourself to us alone and not to the world?' To which Jesus replies, 'Anyone who loves me will heed what I say; then my Father will love him, and we will come to him and make our dwelling with him . . .' To believers Jesus and the Father will come though objectively invisible; there is no need like the credulous and superstitious to scan the heavens, or to ask for evidence that would satisfy an unbelieving world.

There is no injunction here to watch as in the other gospels. Love is ever alert and attentive to what the beloved says. To watch is to wait on the word: to hear and obey.

But Christ cannot come unless he goes away. All that is meant by coming and presence, all the wonder and assurance depends on his departure to prepare a place, to make it possible for the disciples to dwell in the enlargements of eternity and live even now in the divine union. We all know that a friend hundreds of miles distant may so dominate our thoughts and hopes that he or she is infinitely nearer than the person sitting beside us. So it is with the Lord. His absence is as his presence.[9] Always coming, he is always here to those who love him and attend his word. And although we may discern no audible voice, except the exposition of scripture, in the liturgy and preaching, or the words of our friends, we should recall what Yves Congar has said, interpreting the Fathers, about 'the Gospel written in the heart', and also what Ignatius of Antioch wrote:

> He who possesses in truth the word of Jesus can hear even its silence, that he may be perfect, that he may do through what he speaks and know through that of which he is silent.[10]

Second, the disciples will do greater works than those of Jesus in his ministry and prayer in his name will always be granted. Most commentators take 'greater' in the sense of more extensive. The powers hitherto confined to one age and place will be revealed far and wide. When Shakespeare died, Ben Johnson said sorrowfully, 'Yesterday he was our very own. Now he is all the world's.' Such confession could have been made with joy by the disciples after the departure of Jesus. In sheer quantity as in universal scope, the works will be greater.

But there is surely also the promise of the release of new energies consequent upon Christ's death. W. H. Cadman sensitively interprets the words to mean that this happens because the union with the Father which until the Passion was Christ's alone is now shared by all believers. 'The real contrast, then, would appear to be between those works which Jesus was able to do on earth while the Passion was still in prospect and those which are possible once his union with believers has become an accomplished fact.'[11]

These 'greater works' are not independent of Jesus. 'Apart from me you can do nothing' (15.5). And the first promise is succeeded by a second: 'Whatever you ask in my name I will do it', implying that any achievement of the disciples will be in answer to prayer, and so given by Christ, the result of the union. They will be entirely dependent on him. This is why petition, asking, is so vital a part of prayer and not merely on the 'lower level'. It is the recognition of our entire dependence on God. But, here, the prayer would seem to be direct to Christ, 'the Father is so to speak by-passed' (Bultmann) as he is not in 16.23 where he is the One to whom requests are made, though there also 'in the name of Jesus'. 'No one comes to the Father except by me.' There is no direct access to God except in Christ's name, no relation to him without Jesus.

The promise has no qualification: 'Whatever you ask in my name I will do it.' But the prayer is concerned with the work of God, not simply with our human needs and desires, often capricious and born of self-interest. And the name of Jesus will exercise a kind of censorship on our prayers. We cannot expect our petitions to be granted if they are incompatible with him. And the end of all is 'that the Father may be glorified in the Son'; not the display of our own gifts or our short-term success in the sight of men, which in an eternal perspective may not be success at all, but that we may lose ourselves altogether as we and all creation are caught up in the worship of God, the adoration of the love which moves the sun and all the stars.

All this is possible only because Christ goes away into the eternal order and we are united in him to the Father through his consecration of himself in the life of faith and prayer. Of this more below, when we come to think of the Lord's own prayer.

Third, the Lord's departure makes possible the gift of the Spirit. It has been said earlier that the Spirit had not yet been given because Jesus was not yet glorified (7.39). No New Testament author states so emphatically as John that the Spirit's bestowal is the consequence of Christ's going away, his glorification through the lifting up on the cross. But then there is no delay; no waiting for Pentecost. The Spirit is breathed upon the disciples on the evening of Easter Day.

Bultmann is right. Easter, Pentecost and Parousia coincide in John's theology.

He corrects the false tendencies of his time in the church – the wilder apocalypticism, the charismatic excess. But he asserts positively that the going away of Christ makes possible the advent of the divine plenitude – to which the later doctrine of the Trinity would give expression. Jesus himself will return. The incarnation is not ended. 'When he rose, his life rose with him.'[12] 'We see Christ incarnate *through* his resurrection; and this because in his glory his work is consummated and made perpetual.' But he comes with the Father, not simply as the Word made flesh, though he remains as such eternally, but in his perfect union with the Godhead; and he has obtained the Holy Spirit, the Paraclete.

All this with no attendant prodigies and portents. The Son of Man does not come on the clouds of heaven. The disciples still live in the world in the midst of persecutions and dire events and calamities such as happened to their Lord. 'The servant is not greater than his Lord.' Yet they are already in possession of their rooms in the Father's house. And the Spirit himself is given by the breathing of one who speaks peace to calm their fears, rather than as a rushing mighty wind.

There are two important corollaries. One to do with the doctrine of God; the other with the idea of the church.

The Fourth Gospel is theocentric. The Father is supreme. Both Son and Spirit, though in perfect union, are subordinate to him. Christianity is neither a Jesus cult – it would be wrong in terms of this Gospel to call believers 'Jesus people' – nor a sect of 'enthusiasts', Montanists, defined as a fellowship of the Spirit. The Father sent the Son to be the Saviour of the world. The Spirit, though released by Christ's glorification and in response to his prayer, *proceeds from the Father* (15.26). The *filioque* clause

of the Nicene Creed in its Western form, which states that the
Holy Spirit proceeds from the Father *and the Son*, while not
indefensible, is not in accord with Johannine theology.

There is, also, in these chapters of St John, that which makes us
hesitate to ascribe divinity to the outward forms of the church, to
describe it as 'an extension of the incarnation', because it has its
inevitable structures in time, or to refer, for instance, to a leading
functionary as the 'Vicar of Christ'. I remember hearing an argument at table during one of the earliest weeks of prayer for unity
I kept, in which a Dominican sought to commend the papacy –
long before Vatican II – by saying that Christ must have his
representative on earth. He was countered by an Anglican, an old-
fashioned evangelical, who referred him to this promise of the
Spirit. *He* is the Vicar of Christ: not Pope but Paraclete.

John would not understand the Anglo-Catholic hymn:

> And still the holy Church is here
> Although her Lord is gone.

Though we may hesitate to accept Käsemann's suggestion that the
Fourth Gospel may have emanated from 'the relic of a conventicle'
rather than the mainstream of emerging Catholicism, the picture
we have is of a small group around a table at once secure against the
world and sent into it, whose strength and witness are derived not
from orders, or canon law or constitutions, but from the unity
which Christ has made possible with the Father.

And to add 'grace upon grace', to reveal a fullness which knows
no bounds, there is the Paraclete too.

The word has a rich connotation. 'Hall-marked by the juridical
sphere' (Bultmann), it means 'advocate', 'council for the defence',
even witness on someone's behalf; hence helper, friend in need,
counsellor, even comforter in the sense of giver both of consolation
and strength. The Holy Spirit is to be all these.

What cannot be too clearly understood is that the Paraclete is
given to the disciples, not to the world. He is not the Creator
Spirit brooding over the cosmos, life of every star and every soul.
The words of John 4.23, 'God is Spirit', refer to the inmost being
of God, invisible, in his essence unknowable, revealed only by the

voice of his Son, the incarnate Word. They are not to be confined to the Paraclete, who is a particular gift from God's being made available through the work of Christ. Nor I think, if we are to follow John, do we pray that the Holy Spirit may guide the rulers of the nations. The world as such cannot receive him. Even Charles Wesley is wrong. 'The promise made to Adam's race' is not the Johannine understanding of the gift of the Spirit.

We begin with the more narrowly legal sense of advocate.

The Paraclete is sent for a forensic purpose; to stand by Christians in their trial and testing in the world. There is no specific assurance as in the Synoptic Gospels (Mark 13.11; Matt. 10.19f.; Luke 12.11f.) that the Holy Spirit will tell arraigned disciples what to say, but the implication is there in the very title. And the Paraclete will convict the world 'of sin and of righteousness and of judgment' (16.8ff.). He is the counsel for the defence who gains a verdict against the world because those subservient to 'the system' have refused the repudiation and deliverance offered by faith in the incarnate Word. He secures the vindication of God and the justification of his ways to men because Jesus has not departed out of the world into oblivion but to the Father; while the evil one who rules the world is once for all condemned by the events of the Passion and the total triumph of God in Christ.

All this happens not by philosophic argument but by legal. The counsel has to convince the jury that his client is not going against the law but upholding it. And the Spirit secures the conviction of the world because he shows that the whole meaning and purpose of life is in the One whom it has rejected and in the way which is he.

The disciples are told three times that the Paraclete is *the Spirit of truth*. And this takes us beyond the sphere of law without entirely deserting it. The sole mission of the Spirit is to reveal what the letter to the Ephesians calls 'the truth as it is in Jesus' (Eph. 4.21). If Jesus is the interpreter of the Father, the Holy Spirit is the interpreter of Jesus. 'He will teach you all things and bring to your remembrance all that I have said to you' (14.25). 'He will bear witness to me' (15.26) – again a hint of the law courts. Charles Wesley, echoing the *Apostolic Constitutions* (c. AD 375), invokes the

Holy Spirit at the eucharist (in a different sense in this hymn from the traditional epiclesis):

> Come Thou witness of his dying
> Come Remembrancer Divine.

John may think of the Spirit as the witness of *all* that Jesus was and did and not simply of Golgotha, though all his works are signs which point to his crucifixion-resurrection and are incomplete in themselves without that reference.

The Spirit will lead the disciples beyond what Jesus has been able to tell them, though not beyond him. Around that table, they cannot comprehend all the meaning of their Lord. Their minds and spirits would be overwhelmed; they would crack as they almost did. Jesus has to exercise a certain 'economy' then and there. Just as early Christian catechumens were instructed in the mysteries of theology and the rich meaning of the sacraments after they had been initiated into the church and made welcome at the Table, so the disciples, already washed and clean in anticipation, had to go through the travail and trauma of the Passion, which would be a perennial dimension of their future lives, before they could attain knowledge of salvation. The Spirit would help them to see the ever-increasing wonder of Christ's reality, as they passed into ever new discoveries and experience, though not without new sufferings.

This is certainly a promise of which the church in every age must lay hold as the gospel moves into all the earth and ever-succeeding ages and civilizations of mankind, while science explores the whole universe. The spirit of truth also guards against human subjectivity running riot with the Christian gospel. Truth is not something I discover for myself through my religious experience, my conversion. John is possibly in disagreement with Matthew at this point. The words of Jesus to Peter after the confession of his messiahship imply that the revelation has come direct from the Father (Matt. 16.17). In John, truth is always revealed by the Spirit. My own voices may deceive me, the spirits I think come from God may be false. They must be tested by the Holy Spirit, who proceeds from the Father and who deals only in the things of Christ, whether he interprets the Jesus of history, or the ever-present Word, or declares 'the things that are to come'. In some sense, the Spirit is tied to the tradition (and the record of it in scripture), and the church, understood as the company of believers.

But this is not all that is contained in this ministry of the word. The heart of it is union, what Puritan writers called 'the mystic union', though they used the word to mean 'mysterious' – beyond all knowledge and all thought, taking us into the very life of God – not the result of contemplation.[13] This is expounded in the allegory of the vine (15.1–8).

This could be a eucharistic address; possibly on the text 'I will drink no more of the fruit of the vine till I drink it new in the kingdom of God' (Mark 14.25; Luke 22.18). Commentators anxious to fix the allegory in a eucharistic setting, think of Jesus and his disciples still at table and these words as meditation over the cup. But here there is no mention of a cup or of wine; the fruit of the vine in the allegory is simply the grapes, not yet crushed, much less fermented.

Older commentators imagined Jesus and his disciples leaving the table, for there are at the end of John 14 words of dismissal: 'Rise, let us go hence.' They would pass, en route to the garden, the carved vine on the Temple gates, which inspired the homily. And since in the Old Testament the vine is a constant symbol of Israel, it could well be that Jesus is saying, 'I am the true, the real, Israel of God', the second Jacob, as Paul says he is the second Adam.

Whether John envisaged Jesus and his disciples away from table and in conversation as they strolled to Gethsemane, or thought of them still in the place where they had eaten supper, which he never calls the 'upper room', we cannot tell. It is more likely that in chapters 15 and 16 we have either an 'alternative last discourse' (Barrett), or another of the evangelist's interpretations of Jesus's parting, addressed to his own church. It is simplest to think that there are two discourses rather than a jumble of texts for ingenious modern editors to sort out. Since the theme of both is the same – the Lord's going to the Father – and similar material, with some exceptions is used, we have drawn from both in the interests of orderly exposition. And the eucharist and its true meaning seem somehow to brood over the words of all the chapters, for they describe the supreme benefits of the Lord's going away as union with the Father through him, which the great sacrament proclaims and conveys.

There is no doubt that the dominating concern here is the life of the disciples in the future. John does not often use analogies from nature and its processes. In 12.24, Jesus refers obliquely to himself as a grain of wheat, a humble figure indeed, yet perhaps like Julian of Norwich's hazel nut, it is 'all that is made'. The vine too has been planted in the earth before it bears fruit. But the concern here is with the branches, with their fruitfulness which depends on their receiving the life of the vine, through closest union, but also by rigorous pruning to cleanse them, not by washing with water, but cutting with a knife. The fruitless branch is taken away.

What matters supremely is the union. 'Abide in me and I in you. As the branch cannot bear fruit of itself except it abide in the vine, so neither can you except you abide in me.' It is not generally appreciated that union with Christ is the essence of Christian faith and life for Calvinism. This is what the Gospel means. Puritan writers recall the other Johannine analogy of bread and water, and also the hypostatic union of the Godhead – the Son of one substance or being with the Father. So Christians are to be 'in Christ', 'as tendrils of the deathless vine'. The union cannot be closer, nor more intense.

This is the holy of holies of the New Testament. Yet it is not a union which annihilates the individual. To be a branch of the vine is not to be as the drop of water in the beautiful saying of the Buddha, who, when he asked how a mere spot in the dust might live for ever, answered his own question and replied, 'When it is cast into the ocean.' Union with Christ is not absorption in the infinite. We retain our identity and our individuality. Yet we receive our whole life from the vine. His life flows through us. We are entirely dependent. Apart from him we can do nothing. And here, in his will, is our peace.

Jesus goes on to speak of his love for his disciples. To abide in him is to abide in his love and to keep his commandments as

obedient individuals. True love always cherishes individuality –
it does not seek to possess and dominate and overwhelm and suck
life into itself, which is why love here is so much more than the
expression of sexuality or desire.

The imperative – 'that you love one another as I have loved
you' – is repeated. And then the declaration that the union is one
of free and independent persons and does not mean the annihila-
tion of the ego. Love is friendship. 'Greater love hath no man than
this that a man lay down his life for his friends . . . You are my
friends if you do the things that I command you . . .'

Is there a narrowing here? Did not Christ die for his enemies,
too, and is not this the greatest love of all?

Truly, John does look to a universal salvation. 'And I, if I be
lifted up from the earth will draw all men unto myself' (12.32).
But perhaps when the evangelist wrote, although the gospel had
won a widening way into the Roman Empire, if not beyond, the
salvation of the world seemed a more remote possibility than for
the author of Acts, or even the intrepid traveller (and prisoner) St
Paul. And the church was itself 'by schisms rent asunder, by heresies distressed', so that what mattered above all else was that
Christians loved one another and were willing to die for one
another even as Christ had done for them.

Friendship is the truest definition of love in the church. If you
want to go Greek, though it is now commonplace and hackneyed,
so often has it been expounded, there are three words for love:
agape, God's love, especially revealed towards sinners, his initiative
in salvation, unmerited and free, not so much an ethical attitude
as self-communication; *eros*, natural human love, necessary for the
continuance of the race and not to be condemned as altogether
carnal, an immense dynamic, passionate desire for union of bodies
(but, at its highest, of minds too), but also the creative urge and
our longing for God; and *philia*, friendship, not without ardour
of desire, but with a knowledge different from that carnal knowledge expressed in the Hebrew (Adam *knew* Eve his wife, for
example); a knowledge which is intellectual, in that it is knowing
about a person, taking an interest in his history, circumstances,
relations, career, psychology, but also spiritual, being aware of

his human motives, but also his life before God. And friendship *acknowledges* a person in his own right, wills the other's good even at loss of one's own, and is ready to die, if necessary, on the other's behalf.

Our sex-obsessed age may go far to make friendship impossible. A little Freudianism makes us cynical and although there is now a healthy openness about sex as well as all the nastiness, crudity and blatant exploitation, and one would not wish to go back to Victorian prudery, or the cruelties of repression, real damage may have been done to friendship between the sexes and among members of the same sex by a destruction of innocence.

The Jesus of all the Gospels made intimate friendships. He did not rebuff physical contact in his earthly life and enjoyed the close companionship of women as well as men; indeed it could be that, within and perhaps beyond the conventions of the age, his friendships were equally with both, though all was open and communal. While one must not be guilty of anachronism, nor interpret the Gospels by the use of romantic imagination, it may be that the relationship of St Francis of Sales and St Chantal in the early seventeenth century affords some comparison. In his *Introduction to a Devout Life* Francis wrote: 'Friendship based on charity, devotion and Christian perfection is the most excellent of all, for it comes from God, is founded on God and will last for ever in God. What a wonderful thing it is to love on earth as we shall love in heaven, to cherish one another in this world as we shall for ever in the next ... for two people sharing their devotion and their devotional aims become one in spirit.'

Within the Lord's love and care of all whom the Father had given him, he had closer rapport with some than with others. The Beloved Disciple is the ideal, the one who returned his friendship with greatest discernment and sensitivity of understanding and mystic apperception. But Jesus loved Peter too, and all the more because he had to bear with his weaknesses, yet saw in him an especial gift of leadership and the vocation to martyrdom.

'You are my friends', but on condition, 'if you do the things which I command you.' There is a demand for obedience here which makes mutuality between Jesus and his own not exactly as it is between two of the disciples themselves. This is not the language of an equal. It is 'strikingly unsentimental' (Charles Smyth). Jesus speaks almost as an oriental king at whose court the friends were distinguished from the servants because they were in the king's counsels. They knew what he was about, they shared his secrets and his plans. It was similar with Abraham, the friend of God (Isa. 41.8; II Chron. 20.7; James 2.23 cf. Wisd. 7.27), from whom God did not hide what he was going to do (Gen. 18.17).

And so with the disciples of Jesus even when he has gone away, in fact still more when he has gone away, for he anticipates the future presence of the Spirit and truth greater than they can at present bear, when he says, 'All that I have heard from my Father, I have made known to you.'

There is no doubt that this emphasis on knowledge comes from a time and a church where 'Gnosticism', that system which claimed to offer the key to knowledge through which was salvation, was all abroad, and attracted many Christians, who were to find the Fourth Gospel especially congenial. '. . . The suggestion is probably correct that the Evangelist used Gnostic terminology with the intention of rebutting gnostic ideas; but the processes by which this goal was reached remain obscure' (Barrett). The Gospel may have encouraged those who sought rapprochement with Gnosticism, whatever the author's intention. We need not linger among these critical questions, important as they are for the history of Christianity. By the time of Irenaeus in the last quarter of the second century the Fourth Gospel had gained canonicity by its use in opposition to non-Christian Gnosticism. We may find that the friendship of Christ is most real to us because it is contingent upon knowledge. Towards the end of the last war, Charles Smyth wrote in comment on this passage:

At first sight this may appear somewhat arid or at least austere: one would have preferred something a little more emotional. And yet I am not sure. When I sat down to write . . . I had reason to believe that one of my favourite pupils had been killed in action. (By the mercy of God, the report proved to be without foundation.) He was not only a favourite pupil: he was also one of my closest friends. In such an hour the compassion of Christ supports us more than we shall ever know. But the thing by which we find ourselves consciously sustained is not feeling, but knowledge. By that force of mental habit which has become a second instinct, we cling for consolation not to religious sentiment but to dogmatic theology. Consider the initial sentence of the Burial Service: 'I am the Resurrection and the Life: he that believeth in me, though he were dead, yet shall he live: and whosoever liveth and believeth in me shall never die.' That is dogma: and psychologically the approach is absolutely right. Take away from the Christian man his knowledge of the mind of Christ, his initiation into the mystery of the Divine purpose, and how frail and unsubstantial are the consolations of his religion![14]

In spite of this, the disciples of Jesus will have tribulation in the world. He cannot promise that the world will not hate them or be easily won over. Dire things will happen, indeed had happened when the Fourth Gospel was written.

They will put you out of the synagogues; indeed the hour is coming when whoever kills you will think he is offering service to God. And they will do this because they have not known the Father, nor me (16.2,3).

But, as Mark says, the days will be shortened. Just as Jesus parts from them for a little while from his death on the cross to Easter morning, so their own sufferings will not be prolonged. This is a translation of conventional primitive eschatology. The Lord shortens the days because even in the midst of persecution, and the almost limitless agony inflicted in this world, the Risen Christ is with them, the Paraclete strengthens and supports them and the suffering seems as nothing to the joy. It is like a woman's travail in childbirth, except that sometimes the Christian's sorrow, even at its most desperate, is shot through with joy, and as Jesus and his disciples went singing to the Mount of Olives, so, in the succession of faith, there has always been an echo of the triumph song of heaven even in the valley of the shadow of death. Jesus bequeathes peace and joy. In their deepest despair and doubt, the disciples

have the certainty that he has overcome. What they have to do is
to carry on his victory:

> Courage! your captain cries
> Who all your toil foreknew
> Toil ye shall have; yet all despise,
> I have o'ercome for you!

Those around the table seem suddenly convinced. But Jesus does
not welcome their new-found assurance, their sudden, confident
profession of faith. He mistrusts their quick change of emotion.

> To them, the hour of direct communication appears to have
> arrived, for they now believe themselves to be confronted by,
> and, indeed, to be actually apprehending, the revelation of the
> truth of God. At once Jesus answers, 'Behold the hour cometh,
> yea, is come, that ye shall be scattered, every man to his own,
> and shall leave me alone'. An event in history we call the passion
> of Christ, his isolation and death, will have a catastrophic effect
> upon his disciples and throw their new-found confidence
> entirely into question. Yet this is no merely negative demolition
> in the interests of agnosticism or cynicism. *The Father is with
> him.* And his words have been spoken to them so that they may
> receive peace and the joy of Christ's victory. His words *are* the
> means of glory, but neither apart from, nor on this side of, his
> death.[15]

All Christians, most of all in the midst of exuberance, must face
the cross. They will not attain the constancy of union, nor abide
in the vine, unless in some form they have been through the
Passion of Christ. The thought here is not that Christ's disciples
must bear the cross with him, much less that their sufferings can
fill up what is lacking in his (Col. 1.24), or that somehow they
may console him as they try to share his work. He alone can carry
the cross. Rather they have to be made aware of their own weakness and inadequacy in which, as in the crucifixion itself, the
strength of God is made perfect (cf. II Corinthians 12). Cleansed
by the exposure of ultimate reality which the dying of Jesus makes
possible, they will be changed by what he has done so that they

too will endure to the end. There must be radical conversion, which starts with the knowledge that our confident certainties, our greatest achievements, our highest aspirations, our holiest prayers, lead only to the place of a skull. Yet it is there that we are united to the Father and Christ leads us into the eternal order and procures all that we need for our fidelity and our mission.

John does not say so, but we are confronted with this in every eucharist. There is reconstituted the crisis of our redemption. Before ever we talk of 'celebration' we should remember that we are confronted by the cross on which Jesus hangs alone, deserted by those who have professed their insight and their loyalty. And our only hope and our salvation is that the Father is with him. There is our peace and there our cheer.

4 The Prayer of 'Consecration'
John 17

Bishop Westcott called this chapter the Prayer of Consecration. A more familiar title has been the 'High-Priestly Prayer', which is found in the writings of a sixteenth-century Lutheran, David Chytraeus, though it really goes back to Cyril of Alexandria and the Fathers. But ideas of sacrificial atonement are not explicit in the prayer, nor does Christ cast himself in the role of the heavenly Aaron. The verb *hagiazein* in verses 17 and 19 means to separate from the profane, to bring into the sphere of the sacred, that is to sanctify as in the Authorized and Revised versions. It is not often used of a sacrifice, but some commentators think that it has this meaning in verse 19, when Jesus says '*For their sakes* (on behalf of them) I sanctify myself' and therefore modern renderings, like the Revised Standard Version and the New English Bible, prefer 'consecrate'. There is nothing of high-priesthood here, but Barnabas Lindars argues that 'the preposition *huper* (on behalf of) unmistakably introduces a sacrificial connotation. John has used it in the context of laying down one's life in the Shepherd allegory (10.11, 15–18), in the unwitting prophecy of Caiaphas (11.51ff.) and in the Vine allegory (15.13). He has also used it in an allusion to the eucharistic words of Jesus in 6.51.'

Hoskyns, who notes the stress on the ceremonial posture of prayer ('These things spake Jesus and lifting up his eyes to heaven, he said, Father . . .' cf. Pss 123.1; 121.1), continues:

The prayer is the solemn consecration of himself in the presence of his disciples as their effective sacrifice; it is his prayer for glorification in and through his death; it is his irrevocable dedication of his disciples to their mission in the world, and his prayer that both they and those who believe through their teaching may be consecrated to the service of God; and finally, it concludes with the prayer that the Church thus consecrated may at the End behold the glory of the Son and dwell in the perfect love of the Father and the Son.[1]

We may question whether it is not anachronistic and un-Johannine to describe Christ's own, his disciples, in ecclesiastical terms as the church, but the synopsis of the prayer stands. Hoskyns says later that the words of verse 19, 'For their sakes I consecrate myself', are John's interpretation of Mark 14.22–5:

> And as they were eating, he took bread, and blessed, and broke it and gave it to them, and said, 'Take; this is my body.' And he took a cup, and when he had given thanks he gave it to them, and they all drank of it. And he said to them, 'This is my blood of the covenant, which is poured out for many.'

This is a bold leap. Bultmann thinks that John 17 replaces the institution of the sacramental meal, since he believes that John counters the notion that the disciples 'are to be a sacramental fellowship flooded through with heavenly powers'; but at least he admits that there are shared sacrificial ideas between the two evangelists. And since 'This is my body' in the eucharistic words means 'This is I myself', it is not altogether far-fetched to maintain that they are in some sense paraphrased when the Lord prays to the Father, 'For their sakes I consecrate myself.'

Not that this prayer is in any sense a so-called consecration prayer for a eucharist liturgy. It has hardly any of the classic elements first seen in the *Apostolic Tradition of Hippolytus* (c.215, though pieced together from later translations). It is not a prayer for congregational use. There are remarkable parallels of phraseology and theology between it and the thanksgivings reproduced in the *Didache* (The Teaching of the Twelve Apostles), the dating of which has been controversial, but which is now thought to be primitive, and possibly to emanate from the kind of conventicle which Käsemann thinks may be the provenance of St John:

We give thanks to you, our Father, for the holy vine of your child David, which you have made known to us through your child Jesus; glory to you for evermore.

We give thanks to you, our Father, for the life and knowledge which you have made known to us through your child Jesus; glory to you for evermore.

As this broken bread was scattered over the mountains and when brought together became one, so let your Church be brought together from the ends of the earth into your kingdom; for yours are the glory and the power through Christ Jesus for evermore.

We give thanks to you, holy Father, for your holy name which you have enshrined in our hearts, and for the knowledge and faith and immortality which you have made known to us through your child Jesus . . . Remember, Lord, your Church, to deliver it from all evil and to perfect it in your love.[2]

It is interesting that neither in the *Didache* nor in John 17 is there any *direct* mention of the death of Jesus; but John's is not a prayer of thanksgiving over cup and bread, nor is the unity, prayed for so memorably in the *Didache*, precisely that of this chapter.

The prayer indeed is in a class by itself. It is set down as the Lord's own prayer and could not be prayed by anyone else, unlike the Lucan and Matthaean 'Our Father'. It does bear some resemblance to those free prayers which have so often been sneered at as 'sermons to the Almighty'; and it is a prayer to be overheard.

No one has sought to penetrate into it more deeply than the seventeenth-century Calvinist, Thomas Goodwin, who was the chaplain who assured the dying Cromwell that it was not possible to fall from grace. Goodwin's exposition is entitled 'The Heart of Christ in heaven towards sinners on earth', and it has been observed that here is a Puritan devotion towards the Sacred Heart of Jesus, though in the sense of his 'intérieur' rather than that which adores the ruptured organ of his human body and seeks to comfort him in his afflictions. Goodwin finds in the prayer the loving care of Jesus for his own and for him it proves that 'God may be forever said to be compassionate as a man'. He dares to claim that the incarnation 'adds a new way of being merciful: it assimitates all these mercies of God and makes them the mercies of a man'. He anticipates the Victorian hymn:

> Thou knowest, not alone as God all knowing
> As man our human weakness thou hast proved
> On earth with purest sympathies o'erflowing
> O Saviour thou has wept and thou hast loved;
> And love and sorrow still to thee may come
> And find a hiding-place, a rest, a home.

Jesus longs for his disciples to have the joy of heaven. The love of the Father in the union of the Godhead is not enough for him. 'I have thy company but I must have theirs too'.

For Goodwin, the prayer is 'a platform of Christ's heavenly intercession' and it must be admitted that he conflates John and *Hebrews*. For him this is the 'High-Priestly Prayer'.

Yet he may be right in interpreting it, 'in the author's perspective, as the perpetual prayer of the ascended Christ'. John certainly wanted the Christians of his circle, around the table in the community to which he belonged, to believe that Christ was praying for them too like this. 'And not for these only do I pray but for those who believe in me through their word' (17.20).

My Mother was a Methodist class-leader and one day, as a youth, I was looking through her meeting note-book of some years before. She had been expounding John 17 and in her own clear and shapely hand, so much more decipherable than her son's, she had written that she believed that in those words, Jesus had prayer for *her*.

The Fourth Gospel is of such perennial relevance and power because it gives assurance of the work of Christ, which is finished, yet also continuing, so that he is 'no dead fact stranded on the shore of the oblivious years', nor someone whose coming we await, but our present, praying Lord. He intercedes for his own in everything concerned with them when he is gone. They are menaced by the world both in its hostility and its seductions. They may be both persecuted and made to compromise with secularity. Across the street when John wrote was the powerful,

accepted Synagogue towards which Christians felt affinities for
'Salvation is of the Jews' (4.22), but which had rejected angrily
any overtures, and might at any time invoke the powers of the
state against them. There were the hosts of pagans who might lure
them back to the old, indulgent life with its orgies and idolatries,
carefree love of pleasure, and ultimate despair. And within there
might be apostates and traitors and those who deeply misunderstood and misrepresented the things concerning Jesus in the interests of what they deemed 'knowledge', insight into the mysteries
of the universe and eternal salvation. And Jesus prays, not that his
disciples be taken out of the world but that they may be delivered
from evil. He prays calmly, not with 'passionate intensity', nor
'with strong crying and tears'; he is very certain of himself, as
throughout, 'knowing that the Father had given all things into his
hands, and that he had come from God and was going to God'
(13.3); and the depth of his love is the greater because of his
serenity.

Goodwin was right in perceiving that the Jesus who prays 'stands
on the other side of his finished work'. And yet he speaks of his
hour; a recurring theme throughout the Gospel, and it is always
the hour of crisis, the hour determined by the Father which must
not be precipitated before time, the hour welcomed more than
dreaded, the hour of death and of glory, the hour of his return to
God, which will but appear to separate him from those he loves
in the world, but will in fact make possible absent union in a life
that spans both earth and heaven too. 'Father, the hour has come'
(17.1).

R. H. Lightfoot believed that the Apocalyptic Discourse, Mark
13, drawn from Jewish sources, was the evangelist's deliberate
preface to the Passion narrative which immediately follows. We
may say (*pace* Bultmann) that John 17 has a similar place in the
Fourth Gospel. It gives the clue to the Passion in two respects.

1. The Johannine Passion shows the care of Jesus for his own.
He is careful to lose none of them and in the hour of his death he
acknowledges the group beneath the cross and gives his mother
and beloved disciple each to the other. In the prayer all his concern
is for them. No one dare apply the *Lamentations* to the tortured

and crucified Christ of St John. 'Is it nothing to you all you who pass by? Behold and see if there be any sorrow like unto my sorrow.' This Jesus does not seem to be much afraid for himself. He groans because of the unbelief of the Jews at the tomb of Lazarus; he is momentarily troubled that the corn of wheat must fall into the ground and die before there can be a harvest and debates aloud as whether he should ask to be spared his hour, in a seemingly revised version of the prayer of Gethsemane. But he cries instantly,' Father, glorify thy name', and it is the people rather than he himself who require the assuring answer of the heavenly voice, 'I have both glorified it and will glorify it again.' Jesus is agitated because of the treachery of one of his friends and not at peace until Judas has been in some measure exposed and has gone out; and he grieves because of what is going to happen to the faithful weaklings who remain. But he never loses consciousness of his union with the Father. And his prayer for himself is for his disciples, just as he departs out of the world for their inestimable benefit. He consecrates himself and lays down his life, not to pay the price of sin, nor as a ransom or substitute, nor even that God may reconcile the world to himself (though there is a hint of this in 3.16 and 12.32), but for their sakes.

2. The crucifix is no proper representation of the death of Jesus according to St John. For this Gospel, the preoccupation with the sufferings of Christ, particularly in the Western church, though it has responded to a deep need of afflicted humanity, has been misplaced.

I was moved recently to hear of a patient in Christie's hospital in Manchester, who out of the terrible brokenness of cancer and its treatment, cried out, 'Christ was on the cross for three hours. I have already been here for three weeks.' A student told me of a husband, watching his wife die, slowly, painfully over months and years, who similarly contrasted the brevity of Christ's sufferings with hers – and his.

It is true of Jesus that

> We may not know, we cannot tell
> What pains he had to bear.

Time is relative and Christian faith has claimed that his agony was immeasurable. 'He descended into hell.' The Moody and Sankey hymn about the lost sheep may well interpret the Marcan cry of dereliction:

> And none of the ransomed ever knew
> How deep were the waters crossed,
> Or how dark was the night which the Lord passed through
> 'Ere he found the sheep that was lost.

There is also Horace Bushnell's phrase about 'the cross eternal in the heart of God' and the whole of Aberlardian theology, together with Pascal's saying quoted earlier, 'Jesus will be in agony until the end of the world.'

But John is not interested in the quantity of Christ's sufferings nor in any comparisons. For him, death by crucifixion, hideous as it was, is not fulfilling a certain tally of grief and pain so that Jesus must be seen to have suffered more than any other human being. True the Baptist cries at the outset, 'Behold the Lamb of God who takes away the sin of the world.' These words remain without echo in the Gospel, except in the implication that Jesus dies as the lambs are being slaughtered for the Passover. The whole tenor of these last chapters is to explain the purpose of the Passion as the drawing of his disciples and those who will believe in him through their word into the very life of God. In the language of the *Te Deum* – which imagery John does not use – 'to open the kingdom of heaven to all believers'. His death is sacrificial, but not primarily to propitiate, or expiate (in spite of I John 2.2). It is the positive, affirmative triumphant means whereby his own may enter the divine glory which he already shares, and by his death resumes in its eternal fullness.

But John 17 is a prayer and it fulfils the old definition, indebted to Greek philosophy, that prayer is the ascent of the mind to God, or as an Orthodox staretz said, to stand before God with the mind in the heart. This is no more wordless contemplation than it is the imparting of information the Father has no need to hear. It is a conversation and a string of requests within the union of the Son and the Father.

Some have been puzzled at the thought of God praying to himself. This fails to reckon with the subtle sense in which Jesus, though fully God as God may be known, is in this Gospel subordinate to the Father; but even more it misunderstands the nature of prayer as the communion of persons and therefore the very life of God. Prayer is communion *with* God for us; it is the communion *of* God, of the Father and the Son, into which we are drawn. And in that communion asking has its part. No one reading John 17 (or the synoptic Lord's Prayer for that matter) dare say that petition belongs to the 'lower levels' of prayer. It is the highest activity of all. For us it demands the deepest trust. Paul says that to cry 'Abba, Father' is the work of the Spirit of adoption (Romans 8.16). For Jesus it is the sign of the perfect union of love.

True, asking may be the instinctive cry of those far from God who are in trouble. It is like the barking of a dog or the mewing of a cat for food. Perhaps we should not despise the prayers of those who in despair rather than faith cry to God for help; though we must beware of a sentimentality which ignores the need for 'costing choice' and offers an easy road to heaven.

There is an incident recounted by Dietrich Bonhoeffer in *Letters and Papers from Prison*. During a heavy bombing raid when Bonhoeffer was a prisoner they were all lying on the floor: 'someone exclaimed "O God, O God" (he is normally a very flippant type), I couldn't bring myself to offer him any Christian encouragement or comfort; all I did was to glance at my watch and say, "It won't last more than ten minutes now." '[3]

Bonhoeffer did not believe that the man was offering real prayer. D. Z. Phillips who quotes the story in *The Concept of Prayer* also refers to something that he himself overheard:

I heard a diver tell of an experience which occurred while he was searching a wreck. He lost his torch and could not find the exit of the hold. He prayed 'O God get me out of this. I'll do anything you want if only you'll let me find my way out.' Compare that prayer with, 'Yea though I walk through the valley of the shadow of death, I will fear no evil; for thou art with me' (Ps. 23).[4]

Bonhoeffer and Phillips are perhaps a little hard. Some would see even in prayer like this the divine spark in the worldly and careless. One wants to show sympathy to all human urges towards God from out of the miseries of life. But is such prayer more than a spell or incantation, though not altogether foolish? Roman religion at its highest relegated prayer to asking God for what was desired for material prosperity. 'We do not pray to Jupiter', said Cicero, 'to make us good, but to give us material benefits.' 'All men acknowledge that every material good and all material prosperity come from the gods, but no one has ever referred to God the acquisition of virtue. For it is on account of our virtue that we are with justice praised, it is in our virtue that we legitimately glory; which would not be the case if virtue were a gift from God and not an achievement of our own. Therefore we must pray to God for the gifts of fortune, but wisdom we must acquire for ourselves.'

How different was the Gospel from the noblest religion of the world into which it came! The petition of Jesus on behalf of his disciples is not as the naive words of the 'natural man'. Jesus asks, in his perfect union with the Father, for his followers' *sanctification*, which is not the result of their own self-conscious disciplined efforts but of what God will give, in co-operation with their faith and obedience.

He does ask for their protection from the world and he needs to ask because so much can go wrong. The ascent of Jesus to the Father does not guarantee immunity from suffering, persecution or apostasy. Disciples will be in danger. The world is very evil.

No one in this century has understood this better than Sir Edwyn Hoskyns, biblical theologian and commentator on the Fourth Gospel. He spoke with the realism of the Jesus of John 17 to an audience predominantly male in the chapel of Corpus Christi College, Cambridge, in the years between the wars:

You are not to dream through life; you are not to wander about with no roots anywhere; you are not cosmopolitan gentlemen floating about; you are grounded in the earth, men of the world. That is, however, but one side of the truth. We can be overwhelmed by the world, crushed by it, in bondage under its elements. But we are Christians engaged in a struggle between the flesh and the spirit, called to be sons of God by Christ, in the world, yet not of it. We do not worship a disembodied spirit. We worship the Christ. We eat his body and drink his blood (crude though the language may seem, the truth of the Christian religion is there). Flesh and blood controlled by the Spirit of God and brought into submission to the will of God is the life of the Church. And this is your salvation and mine, a salvation grounded upon a tension which is never resolved in this life.

But Christian hope, based upon belief in God and upon the return of Jesus to the Father, declares that the tension will be resolved, not by death but in life eternal. 'In my Father's house are many mansions; if it were not so, I would have told you.' But more important words for us here and now run thus: 'I pray not that thou shouldest take them out of the world, but that thou shouldest keep them from the evil ... Sanctify them through thy truth.'[5]

Jesus does not pray for the world, which is disturbing for universalists and seems to limit both the scope of his intercession and the life of his disciples. But for John there is a sense in which the only hope for the world is that it cease to be the world. Therefore it cannot be prayed for as it is. It is not wholly left out. There is an oblique prayer for the world (Hoskyns) in that the purpose of the community of the disciples for which Jesus asks is that the world may believe and know that the Father has sent him. This is not simply that the world may recognize him, though possibly too late, as in the Wesley hymn based on the Apocalypse:

> Every eye shall now behold him
> Robed in dreadful majesty;
> Those who set at nought and sold him,
> Pierced and nailed him to the tree,
>   Deeply wailing
> Shall the true Messiah see.

'God so loved the world that he gave his only begotten Son, that whosoever believeth in him should not perish but have eternal life.' That may be 'a traditional Christian formula which the evangelist employed' (Käsemann); but it cannot be left out of the reckoning in any attempt to grapple with the paradox of the Johannine attitude to the world.

The disciples can only share in the divine mission to the world and mediate the divine love for the world as they 'are kept pure in unworldly existence'. As Bultmann says, the prayer for protection is the same as the prayer for holiness. 'Holy Father, keep them in thy name which thou has given me . . .' (17.11). 'The name of the Lord is a strong tower' (Prov. 18.10). This name is the word which God has given Jesus to utter; it is the revelation. Therein is security; in the Holy Name, not invoked as in a cult but as the whole life of the community is enveloped in the Divine disclosure made in Christ.

And so the prayer becomes a prayer for unity:

> Holy Father, keep them in the name which thou hast given me, that they may be one, even as we are one (17.11).
>
> I do not pray for these only, but also for those who believe in me through their word, that they may all be one; even as thou Father art in me and I in thee, that they also may be in us, so that the world may believe that thou hast sent me (17.20, 21).
>
> The glory which thou hast given me I have given to them, that they may be one even as we are one. I in them and thou in me, that they may become perfectly one, so that the world may know that thou hast sent me and hast loved them even as thou hast loved me (17.22, 23).

These words have become the charter and inspiration of the ecumenical movement, which William Temple, over forty years ago, described as 'the great new fact of our era', and which, especially through the Second Vatican Council, has made incredible advances since, though it is in some measure halted now. Reaction is widespread, and there are new divisions or old ones rampant as ever. In spite of much theological discussion and a plethora of 'schemes', which have achieved visible success in reconciling episcopal and non-episcopal churches only in India, there is still confusion as to the unity we seek. Is it Catholic unity, in the sense of the historic churches of Europe and the Middle East, a 'vision glorious' of the mystical body of Christ on earth, which founders because of differing notions of the authority which alone could translate it into the actualities of life in the world? And while these churches and their offshoots still talk or suspend talks, they decline, in strength and often in public influence, and the vitality of the church is manifest in sects who lack the vision, or in the teeming churches of Africa and their derivatives who multiply without being organically one, though those who observe them often find great warmth of love. There are also those who, not without a whiff of Marxism, would find unity in action against injustice, on behalf of the poor, the oppressed, the victims of racialist and capitalist tyranny. Their banner might be inscribed with the device that in Christ there is neither Jew nor Greek, slave nor free, male nor female; 'for you are all one in Christ Jesus' (Gal. 3.28). If they have any interest in Catholicity – the unity of the one authentic church which goes back to the beginning and, in Christ, to the foundation of the world, and is one with the whole company of heaven as well as visible here on earth, they would re-define it, and not allow us to forget that 'here we watch and struggle and here we live in hope'.

None of these diverse patterns corresponds to the unity for which Jesus prays according to St John. This unity is a sharing in the very life of God. It is not the same as the Pauline declaration 'you are all one in Christ Jesus'; it goes beyond Christ to the Father; it is to have part in the mutual indwelling of the Father and the Son . . . 'that they may all be one even as thou Father art in me and I in thee, that they also may be in us'.

This carries us into realms different from those of the practical theology which tends these days to dominate our Christian lives. It is not easy to say what it means in this-worldly terms because it seems to remove the friends of Jesus totally to the sphere of the divine glory. (Käsemann can even write of 'the metaphysical dimension'.) Yet it offers the only hope for the church on earth.

Our unity begins in God, who is one, not simply in that he is over against the multiplicity of idols, 'gods many and lords many', though there is great courage to be gained from that. He is one in himself in the union of perfect love, expressed here as that of Father and Son, and all our Christian life begins – and ends – there, not in order, not in the kiss of peace, nor in good comradeship in mission, but in the unity of God. It is love as he is love, yet so far transcendent that our human experience of loving is an imperfect parable indeed. In the prayer love is the last word, not the first, yet all comes to rest here, 'this complex of personal communication and dialogue between the Father and the Son, their reciprocity of will and being and possessions, their disposition and act of giving, their mutual indwelling and their unity'. 'The love of the Father for the Son from before the foundation of the world embraces the disciples.'

This is where our unity begins and if we would see this Lord's Prayer answered we should start not with conferences and constitutions nor theological debates, but in prayer as Jesus prayed. We should come together, irrespective of our labels and allegiances and together seek union with God by waiting on his word. There will be differences of interpretation, dialogue may mean argument, but we shall find each other only as we find our unity in him.

This is why the desire for spiritual ecumenism, represented by the first gathering of British church leaders at Canterbury in April 1984 for agendaless 'recollection' – and surely seen by Pope John Paul II as the way forward in spite of his desire to re-appraise Vatican II and the scant possibility of intercommunion, or those changes which would allow the priesthood of women or clerical marriage – is our great hope. It will not spare us the patience and the pain of working out how the scattered people of God may become institutionally one in the world. That must still be an aim; it would seem to be a necessity if Catholic Christianity is to survive; but it will never be perfectly achieved in this age and we must reckon with those tensions in which Christians in church and out of it will always have to live. First let us lift up our eyes to heaven and not glance ever at one another to see if our orders are valid or our doctrine 'sound'. These are not things 'indifferent' and we cannot evade them by an escape into 'spirituality'; but they are not where unity begins. Our union is with the Father and with his Son Jesus Christ. As his life and love flow into us we shall be reconciled amid the imperfections of life on earth and partakers, even now, of the heavenly glory, which comprehends in true Catholicity all the gifts of the ascended Christ to his people.

But this unity in the truth which is so much vaster than our most authentic grasp of it, and the holiness which both separates us from the counterfeit values of an evil and passing world, and helps us to love as Christ loves us, is possible only because of the sacrifice of the intercessor. 'For their sakes I consecrate myself.' He has gone to his glory through the laying down of his life on the cross. And in the blessed sacrament he gives us his very self and all the benefits of his Passion. 'This is my body . . . This is my blood.' 'For their sakes I consecrate myself.' *We* do not consecrate ourselves. This is the prayer of Christ and Christ alone. There is no parallel in our lives.

> He only could unlock the gate
> Of heaven and let us in.

We do not consecrate Christ in the eucharist, nor offer him over again. But even as we eat and drink we enter with him into his glory, and although we must return to the tensions and compromises of the world, we shall not only be kept safe from evil, we shall possess already our inheritance in eternal life and abide in the unity 'into which all the friends of the Crucified are to be made perfect'.[6]

5 Crucifixion — Resurrection — Communion
John 18, 19, 20

'As often as you eat this bread and drink this cup, you show forth the Lord's death until he come' (I Cor. 11.26). That is Paul's teaching about the Lord's Supper, and in both his tradition and John's there must be more than word and prayer and more than ritual act, however solemn and central. The eucharist is a proclamation of the death of Christ and has meaning only because that took place. The communion, the eating and drinking, the participation in holy things, is the consequence of his departure from this life in violent and cruel circumstances. So John, who does not describe an institution at a meal, makes it entirely clear that the One who consecrates himself in prayer, possibly while still at table, must go out and face arrest, trial and death by crucifixion – a death the reality of which cannot be disputed for he is pierced to the heart as well as nailed to the cross, and, though right royally, is buried as buried could be.

There are certain especial characteristics of the Johannine Passion.

1. Jesus is always in control, the heavenly being before whom his apprehenders fall awestruck. 'When he said to them "I am he" they drew back and fell to the ground' (18.6). There is no hint of the psychological effect of an overwhelming personality. This is the final 'I am' (ego eimi) saying, with its divine claims.

He seeks his disciples' freedom; he is more concerned than ever with them rather than himself. He will not let them defend him. 'The cup which the Father has given me, shall I not drink it?' (18.11). This is the one mention of the cup either at supper or in the garden. Before his disciples can drink of the cup (cf. Mark

10.38, 39) he must drain it. It is the cup of the Lord's anger against sin, but whereas the psalmist says that it is the wicked who shall drink it to the dregs (Ps. 78.9), all the Gospels make this the vocation of the Son of Man.

> How bitter that cup
> No heart can conceive
> Which he drank right up
> That sinners might live!

In the Judgment Hall, Jesus does not argue or seek to justify himself. He is almost detached, allowing pre-ordained events to take their course. He makes declarations as to the nature of his kingship and authority, but he asserts that Pilate is only able to condemn and crucify him because he has been given for the purpose the authority of God and is in some sense a puppet in the divine control. Those who have given Jesus over to Pilate – and, though the singular is used, this means not simply Judas but those elements in the Jewish nation who rejected and hated Jesus – are the people responsible, guilty of sin, for they are not the impartial, if woefully imperfect, administrators of justice, they have asserted their wills against the truth of God and become servants of the Father of lies.

We may note in passing that there is here a possible adumbration of a doctrine of the state, though it is not a parallel to Romans 13.1ff., 'The powers that be are ordained of God'. But Pilate stands in a neutral position between God and the world and is not condemned as the world is. His very existence is not like that of the world, rebellion against God. Better that Jesus should be brought before a Roman procurator, albeit one with a reputation for callousness and brutality, a perpetrator of blunders and atrocities, than that he should be altogether the victim of mob rule. Pilate has responsibility. And he makes efforts to release Jesus. He may genuinely believe that the crowd will prefer Jesus to Barabbas, a bandit, or take pity on a tortured and humiliated man, not a criminal type, with nothing fearsome in his appearance now except what men have done to him, a pathetic victim of brutal horse-play. The least he expects is that they will in cacophonous chorus protest their loyalty to the hated Caesar and repudiate this strange prophet of their own race. Pilate's failure in the trial of Jesus is that, like so many politicians, he is not interested in truth, either as ultimate reality or moral principle; merely in what is expedient. Even so, he is in his weakness the instrument of a will totally beyond his comprehension and vaster than the empire which he represents.

In all this, Jesus is not the prisoner but the judge. Pilate himself is tried and found wanting; the enemies of Jesus are totally condemned.

On the way to Golgotha, Jesus bears his own cross. There is no *via dolorosa*, no place for any 'stations of the cross', no Simon of Cyrene. On the cross, Jesus reigns as king and Pilate seeks to redeem his weak submission to the mob by placarding the fact, and in the three languages of that civilization. 'Pilate also wrote a title and put it on the cross; it read "Jesus of Nazareth, the King of the Jews" . . . and it was written in Hebrew, in Latin and in Greek' (19.19, 20). This is an unwitting declaration of a rule wider than that over Israel. 'Pilate, therefore, contrary to knowledge and intention, has become a prophet' (Bultmann).

The crucifixion is then an enthronement. Jesus reigns from the tree. He does not lose consciousness, nor appear 'a man of sorrows, acquainted with griefs', deranged by suffering. The thirst is recorded not to call attention to the distresses of crucifixion, but as in fulfilment of scripture, to show that all things are moving to a divine consummation, the finishing of the Father's work. 'The cup that my Father has given me shall I not drink it?' Jesus remains totally in charge, making provision for his friends and in death triumphant. All is kingly, all is calm.

There may be a hint in St John that Jesus is in charge of his own resurrection. The New Testament tradition, the Christian faith, is that God raised him up. But earlier in the Fourth Gospel, Jesus says 'I lay down my life, that *I* may take it up again' (10.17). And here there is no rumour of earthquake. The stone has been removed and the grave clothes lie in order as if the Lord had risen and folded them himself.

2. There is deep irony in it all, just as we have noted in Pilate's

title for the cross. If Pilate there unknowingly proclaims a universal sovereignty, earlier, before the Passion begins, Caiaphas had prophesied in his time-serving counsel of expediency, the vicarious sacrifice. ' "It is expedient for you that one man should die for the people, and that the whole nation should not perish". He did not say this of his own accord, but being high priest that year, he prophesied that Jesus should die for the nation, and not for the nation only, but to gather into one the children of God who are scattered abroad' (11.49f.).

In the Passion itself, there are other ironies of detail. When Pilate said to the crowd 'Here is the man!', he probably meant 'Pity the poor fellow!', tortured, degraded, powerless. In fact, Pilate is declaring that here is the Son of Man, the Proper Man, the One who has taken our humanity upon him and raised it to the right hand of God. When Pilate said, 'Here is your King!' he pointed to a pathetic spectacle, divested of all earthly glory, but, as in the title, he prophesied the reign of truth. The thirst too is not without irony. He who is the living water dies athirst and it is thus that the living water flows out into all history.

There are other ironies, which, whether so obviously intended or not, may be discerned. There is the extravagance of the burial. John says that Jesus was embalmed according to Jewish custom, not Egyptian, which involved mutilation of the body. Nicodemus, who had first visited Jesus by night (John 3) provided a lavish mixture of myrrh and aloes, more than half-a-hundred weight, to give a strolling preacher who lived communally with his disciples a burial fit for a king.

There must be a certain extravagance about Christian devotion.

> Give all thou canst! High heaven rejects the lore
> Of nicely calculated less or more.

This, humanly speaking, keeps the memory of Christ and his beauty alive, throughout the world and throughout the ages, just as the perfume of the ointment filled the house at Bethany and the garden tomb in the place where he was crucified. Christianity could not survive on earth, so it would seem by our reckoning, if there were not those whose love for him pervades society and may in some ways be sensed in whatever form it takes, the sacrifice of life, or the offering of the self in visible forms of devotion. As Paul Gerhardt's hymn puts it, in Wesley's translation:

> Too much to thee I cannot give
> Too much I cannot do for thee;
> Let all thy love and all thy grief
> Graven on my heart for ever be.

But the irony is that all the devotion of converted sinners and sanctified saints, of apostles and martyrs from the greatest to the least, and of those who long even out of timidity and partial understanding to love him more, cannot do more than bury Jesus, bury him with reverence so that his life is not forgotten, his memory remains and does not lose its power. But no more than Nicodemus's weighty mixture of myrrh and aloes can our devotion raise the dead.

The greatest irony of all lies in the saying to Martha at Bethany. 'I am the Resurrection and the life.' How can the Resurrection die? How can he whose voice has power to call the dead from the tombs himself be 'crucified, dead and buried'? Yet this is what must happen of divine necessity and, according to John, the immediate cause of it is the raising of Lazarus. Irony upon irony! How can the Resurrection die? Yet would he be the *Resurrection* if he had not undergone death? Resurrection is not immortality. As Pascal said, 'It is there in the sepulchre that Christ takes on new life.' Or Paul Tillich:

> The new life would not really be *new* life if it did not rise from the complete end of the old. Otherwise it would have to be buried again. But if the new life has come out of the grave, then the Messiah himself has appeared.[1]

By his description of Lazarus stumbling out of the tomb still bound in the wrappings of the corpse, John 'is ironically reminding his readers that very soon they will realize if they follow the story to the end that this is not "the real thing". Rather it is an episode that must take place in order that the substance as distinct from the shadow of divine omnipotence may be shown.' Hence, in contrast, the folded grave clothes of Easter morning.

The death of Jesus in St John is so much the perfect work that one sometimes wonders why he needs Resurrection stories. He might, like W. H. Auden, have understood and sympathized with Simone Weil's difficulty. 'If the Gospels omitted all mention of Christ's Resurrection, faith would be easier for me. The cross by itself suffices me.' Is not the cry 'It is finished!' enough? And does not faith, for us, both have its meaning and receive its beatitude because we have not seen the tomb empty, nor been vouchsafed appearances? We have simply the man on the cross laying down his life for his friends and for the scattered children of God, and we must believe through the inward knowledge of his self-giving that this is God's perfect work.

But this will not do for John. The Resurrection implies the reality of the death and its vindication – not reversal. It was not the descent from the cross postponed for thirty-six hours. Jesus loved to *the end* (13.1). This must be seen and understood by the disciples. True, John tells successively what was simultaneous and all contained in the cross; but what from the eternal aspect was all one must be seen as process in the lives of the disciples, in order that they may comprehend both the completeness of their Lord's victory plucked out of real death and shame and the enmity of the world, and that by the very nature of his triumph there will be a new relation to him, which – to echo Hort again – takes its character not from their circumstances but from his, and enables them to possess already the place prepared in the Father's house. But we may agree with Bultmann that the incidents in chapter 20 contain 'a peculiar critique' of those Easter stories in Matthew and Luke in which physical contact is not only allowed but demanded by Christ.

The events recorded in John 18–20 may therefore be described as crucifixion-resurrection, with the hyphen all important. But this makes possible communion and we may understand what this means if we look at the groups and individuals whom John describes.

1. *The group beneath the cross*. There is first the little company at

the foot of the cross. Not all, for John, have forsaken and fled, or stand afar off like the women in Mark. None of the twelve is present unless the beloved disciple be their representative, the one who knows and follows in 'sure and certain hope' while the others are distraught and made cowardly by fear. There were four women – so it would seem – to one man. John may well have been more of a feminist than most in the early church, who, contrary to prevailing custom, entrusted tasks of prominence and leadership to women. Chrysostom may have discerned something of this when he wrote, 'The weaker sex then appeared the more manly, so henceforth were all things transformed.'

What happens here may be seen as the founding of the church, the new family of God. His mother, who is not known in this Gospel by the name Mary, has embarrassed Jesus at the wedding at Cana, and been, if not repudiated ('Woman, what have I to do with you?'), discouraged from interference, though she has some part in the sign. But Jesus seems to disown her as his natural mother, and it is difficult to find in this Gospel any warrant for peculiar honour to be done to her because she bore him. (If we discount the birth stories in Luke and Matthew, this is the synoptic tradition too, e.g. Mark 3.31ff. and parallels; Luke 11.27, 28). But now, when natural relations have been disrupted and ties of flesh and blood dissolved in the crisis of the ministry, Jesus, from the cross, creates a new family. 'Woman, here is your son! . . . . . . Here is your mother!' Perhaps the two are to be seen not as characters in a 'human interest story' but as types, the mother representing Jewish, the disciple, Gentile Christianity (Loisy, Bultmann). But there is nothing of this in the text. It is best to regard the incident as marking the creation of the Christian fellowship of the friends of Jesus, which contains female and male and transcends natural associations and more than makes good their surrender in the communion of saints (cf. Mark 10.28–30). In this company, the mother of Jesus has her place as the one whom he gave to be the mother of his disciple.

2. *The piercing and the witness.* 'From that hour the disciple took her to his own home' (19.27). Some think that this means 'immediately', so that the two departed from the scene. But in that case

who is the witness of the death and piercing? The obvious implication would be the one from whom the author of the Gospel gained his history and interpretation, who if the beloved disciple had left with the mother could not have been he. Or may we say that the Holy Spirit is meant, 'the witness of his dying' after the Apostolic Constitutions and Wesley, mentioned above; he brought these to the remembrance and testimony of later Christians. The first letter of John links the Spirit with the water and the blood: 'There are three who bear witness, the Spirit and the water and the blood and these three agree in one' (I John 5.8). There is also the strange language in which the Fourth Gospel describes the death of Jesus, masked by modern translations, which is literally to be rendered, 'He handed over the Spirit', though, if we read anything into that, we have to presuppose that there were still some of the group beside the cross and that 'from that hour' means 'from the hour of the complete sacrifice of the Christ' (Hoskyns) where 'hour' has the significance of the time of consummation as in so many other instances in this Gospel.

The piercing is of importance for the theology of the Gospel in that it affirms that Jesus truly died, while remaining the unblemished victim. 'Not a bone of him shall be broken.' The breaking of bread in the eucharist was never intended to simulate the brokenness of Christ's body on the cross; it was entirely to make possible the distribution, the sharing.

But behind the Johannine Passion lurks the Jewish Passover. No bone of the paschal lamb shall be broken (Ex. 12.46). And although John does not explicitly mention the detail, his timing of the crucifixion is that at which the lambs were being slain, so that he might agree with Paul: 'Christ our Passover is sacrificed for us; therefore let us keep the feast' (I Cor. 5.7).

The piercing also testifies that life and cleansing flow from Christ's death. There may also be an intended reference to the sacraments of baptism and the Lord's Supper, though blood comes before water, and if this be so, the eucharist precedes baptism. But here on the cross is the bread which is Christ's flesh given for the life of the world, and the blood which must be drunk (John 6.51, 53), and the water through which the Christian passes in his own baptism, which is his new birth from above. Both sacraments have their origin in the death of Jesus and communion is possible only through that.

Toplady's hymn 'Rock of Ages' applies the emission in a slightly different way and from a theology not precisely Johannine.

> Let the water and the blood,
> From thy riven side which flowed,
> Be of sin the double cure,
> Cleanse me from its guilt and power.

Some in our time deplore the individualism of the hymn, so concerned are they for a social gospel. In its heyday it united Mr Gladstone, whose Latin translation of it is carved into a pillar in his parish church at Hawarden, and my paternal grandmother, whom I never knew, but whose last words from her poverty-stricken deathbed in middle age were

> Foul, I to the fountain fly;
> Wash me, Saviour, or I die.

The hymn is the favourite of black congregations in the inner city; it is a song of their experience and takes us back to the *katharsis* of John 13.

'They shall look on him whom they pierced'. The scripture cited is Zech. 12.10, from an Old Testament book which does much to shape the Passion narratives of all the evangelists. The prophet describes someone to whom the people have done despite, a figure as mysterious as the Suffering Servant of Isa. 53. As they mourn for him, the Lord will turn their hearts:

> ... I will pour a spirit of pity and compassion (RSV = compassion and supplication) into the line of David and the inhabitants of Jerusalem. Then
> They shall look on me, on him whom they have pierced, and shall wail over him as over an only child, and shall grieve for him bitterly as for a first-born son.

This is no prophecy of doom but of conversion. The implication in St John may not be that of the Apocalypse:

> Behold he is coming with the clouds! Every eye shall see him and among them those who pierced him; and all the peoples of the earth shall lament in remorse (Rev. 1.7).

If we recall the conversation with Nicodemus and the comparison between the exposure of the brazen serpent in the wilderness and of the lifting-up of the Son of Man on the cross we may feel that the old Salvation Army song gives a valid interpretation:

> There is life for a look at the Crucified One.

But we cannot altogether ignore the lamentation, although, as we have so clearly stated above, the Jesus of St John seeks no pity for himself. The seamless robe suffers the indignity of being taken from the Lord's body and put up in a lottery by the coarse executioners; but they do not rend it. One may contrast Mark Antony's blatant manipulation of the Roman crowd when he holds before them Caesar's torn and blood-stained mantle:

> If you have tears prepare to shed them now!

For John the word would be almost as in Milton's *Samson Agonistes*:

> Nothing is here for tears.

Those who are drawn to the Crucified by the eye of faith may weep for themselves and their sins and the sufferings of humanity, but their union with him and the Father transcends a compassion for himself he does not ask, and tears he does not require.

And although he is wounded to death and his sacred heart laid bare, this is not to arouse pity, much less a desire to be with him and comfort him in his woe. This we cannot do. Though we have never been his deliberate enemies, 'those who set at naught and sold him, pierced and nailed him to the tree', our good deeds may make him suffer as much in his torn wretchedness as our sins.

'They shall look on him whom they pierced.' Yet withal, the sight is not doom-laden but salvific.

Never love nor sorrow was
  Like that my Saviour showed:
See him stretched on yonder cross,
  And crushed beneath our load!
Now discern the Deity,
  Now his heavenly birth declare!
Faith cries out: 'Tis he, 'tis he,
  My God that suffers there!

And we go to the table of the Lord to see this by faith.

3. *The race to the tomb.* Whether or not we think of the mother of Jesus and the beloved disciple as types rather than individuals as they stand beneath the cross, it is hard to avoid the feeling that Simon Peter and the disciple represent different traditions from different centres of the primitive church. This is heightened by the conclusion of the appendix to the Gospel, chapter 21, when Peter, looking over his shoulder at the beloved disciple and wondering if he will outlive him and be spared martyrdom and indeed survive until the Lord comes, is told that he must fulfil his own vocation and not be distracted by speculations about another's fate. There may be here in the mind of the Fourth Evangelist or his editor a challenge to the supremacy of Peter, or even a contention for his own church over against Rome, with which Peter was early associated and which was already asserting that primacy so influential in the development of Western Christendom.

If so, there is no desire to oust or supplant Peter. When they hear from Mary Magdalene that the stone has been moved from the entrance to the tomb, both Peter and the beloved disciple set out running. The other disciple wins the race and gets to the tomb first. He sees that it is empty but does not go in. Simon Peter, catching up, runs on into the tomb and sees the folded grave-clothes, which would seem to be described in deliberate contrast to those which still bound Lazarus (11.44). 'Then the disciple who had reached the tomb first went in too, and he saw and believed.' He came first to the Easter faith, though Peter has a certain precedence in discovery of the outward facts; but the other needed no appearance of the risen Jesus, no argument from scripture; *he saw and believed.*

The one beside whom he had sat at supper, and who from the cross had created through him the new family of the church, had broken the bonds of death. Was it love that made faith possible?

Peter needed more. He had denied Jesus and there must be a personal restoration. He was different from the beloved disciple and God's way with him was different. If we may let fancy roam a little and, against a more rigorous rule, combine the various glimpses we have of him in the New Testament, we may conclude that his denial of Christ brought him to a traumatic conversion; that he became a Pentecostalist and according to Acts, Galatians, St Matthew's Gospel and church tradition, an ecclesiastic. The erst-while enthusiast who has learnt something of his own instability and who is not an intellectual or a mystic with tremendous resources and perceptions within his own heart and mind, may need the support of the institution with its rules of discipline and may resist a too wide tolerance, a too great openness.

The intellectual and the mystic will outrun his fellow; but he will come to a place where he will pause in reverence and wait for Peter to catch up. And before the mystery of what God has done, the fast and the slow, the impatient and the tardy, the contemplative and the active are alike arrested and brought to silent awe. In the end neither has absolute precedence. The crucified-risen Saviour has communion with them and reveals himself according to their needs and in his own ways.

4. *Mary Magdalene.* Christian tradition has seen Mary Magdalene in two roles. She is the living embodiment of the saying, so hard for the respectably religious, that 'the harlots and publicans go into the kingdom of heaven before you'; though Jesus saves her from the demonic element in her sexuality. This is how she appears in *Godspell*. She is also the woman of deep emotion, given easily to tears, inclined to hysteria and depression, Mary *Maudlin*, of whom the great mediaeval hymn about the new Jerusalem says, 'There Magdalene hath left her moan'.

These, however, are inferences drawn from the piecing together of scriptural fragments and of a conflation of differing Gospel accounts. They assume that Mary Magdalene was the woman who anointed Jesus with spikenard and tears; that the unnamed woman

who wept *over* him in Simon the Pharisee's house according to St
Luke, was the one who stood weeping *for* him in the Easter garden
according to St John.

In Luke 8.2 it is said that seven devils had come out of her, which
may suggest mental illness rather than prostitution. The strong
tradition in both Mark and John, though surprisingly not in Luke,
is that she was a spectator of Calvary – at a distance in Mark,
beneath the cross in John, and that she was early at the tomb on the
third day. John gives no hint of her past, how she has come to be
where she is – except that she is a woman friend and disciple of
Jesus, who has not deserted him. She stands distressed in the garden
as one for whom relations with him have dominated her life; and
these have not been abstractly spiritual. Mary demands some
bodily presence. She needs to hear a voice, to see a form, to be
spoken to by name, to enter into conversation and to be able to
express love by physical contact – touch, handclasp, embrace,
words of devotion, giving of gifts.

> O for the touch of a vanished hand
> And the sound of a voice that is still!

But if Jesus is now forever among the dead, Mary wants a grave,
to feel that there is a place on earth where his body lies to await the
resurrection, where she may still show her love, a shrine.

The angels who are now sitting in the tomb, a strange intrusion
into the story at this point, for they had not been seen before, fulfil
no real purpose and must be vestiges of the synoptic tradition, are
unable to help Mary. They do nothing for her at all. But then she
sees Jesus and, like the two on the road to Emmaus in Luke 24,
does not at first recognize him. They know him in the breaking of
the bread, after he has expounded the scriptures – almost a liturgy
of word and sacrament. Mary recognizes him when he speaks her
name. Sight may not bring recognition; it is the voice which
reveals Jesus, no longer dead, the voice of the Good Shepherd who
knows his own by name.

But once she knows that he is alive and is brought to rapturous
joy by the familiar accents which are uniquely for her, Mary, she
has to learn that the friendship cannot be as it was. The individual

presence in the body will be there no longer. This is the last fleeting experience of it.

Those for whom the Fourth Evangelist wrote could not know Jesus as his first followers had done. To try to do so would lead them as it did some in subsequent ages, mystics and others, to excessive use of imagination, to fantasy and eroticism. They would make Christ in the image of the ideal hero of their time, whether mediaeval knight or English gentleman, or handsome lover; or even in their own image. This could result in a cloying and carnal sentimentality, to being in love with Jesus, and a transformation of the strange, numinous figure of the gospels into one with whom they could come to terms.

The obverse danger is to lose sight of Christ's humanity, which is what St John may come near to doing, but not quite.

This may happen apart from any belief that our friends are supernatural beings. We know well that absence makes the heart grow fonder. It is easier to love those at a distance whom we see or hear from occasionally when the whole encounter may be a celebration of friendship, than to retain patience with our constant companions, or associates, or co-inhabitants. In retrospect we may discover a great affection for people whom we found intensely irritating and annoying when we were with them – sometimes because they recall and validate our own past. Death often hallows associations which were far from perfect in life. We have all known those bereaved who have canonized the departed and their relations with them, whereas in life there were as many difficulties as with those who survive. Christian faith is sometimes tested by the thought that Jesus may have been an uneasy and bewildering companion, vivid, exciting, with a compelling power, yet capable of great indignation. Was he always patient at home? Was he not, like any prophet, disturbing? And have not his followers been relieved to have him in high heaven, object of adoration, the apogee of their ideals, to whom they could sing hymns and pay metaphysical compliments, but whose living voice could never interrupt and question and rebuke and recall them to judgment and the love of God and the 'Galilean vision of humility'?

If we would learn the truth about our relations both with Jesus

Christ and with our fellows we must reckon with the incident before us:

> Jesus said 'Mary!' She turned to him and said, Rabboni!' (which is Hebrew for 'My Master!'). Jesus said 'Do not cling to me, for I have not yet ascended to the Father.'

Jesus seems to be telling Mary Magdalene that her longing to resume the old friendship would restrain him from the fulfilment, the consummation, of his destiny in which alone true satisfaction and salvation lie. 'By clinging to me you are preventing me from going to God and the relation between you and me is eternal and life-giving if I am with him. My earthly life was indeed decisive because there the victory of God in human existence was achieved. But that is now accomplished and in some sense over. My validity for you is not in a direct human relationship between the two of us. No! not even in me, Jesus, risen from the dead – it is only as I ascend to the Father, in my presence with him, that yours and mine can be anything other than a human devotion, which may become obsessive, infatuated and idolatrous. Salvation is not a matter of you and me, but of you, me and the Father'.

That Jesus says that he has not yet ascended is a puzzle to some, for John would have us believe that the ascension takes place on Golgotha, the total triumph was then and there. Are we to think that because the Holy Spirit, the gift of his glorification, was breathed upon the disciples later that day, that Jesus ascended between the appearance to Mary Magdalene and his entry through the closed doors to the ten? No; it is in Mary's own experience that the ascension has not taken place, that the events need to be in succession that she may be brought to new understanding.

The harsh truth is that to make human relations the supreme end of life is idolatrous. Stephen Spender, the man of letters, writes very wisely of this in his 1939 September Journal, included in his book, *The Thirties and After*. His own first marriage had broken up, but he is writing specifically of his German friends on the eve of the Nazi take-over. They had 'lived as though nothing mattered except sex and personal relationships'. These last, he says, should be subject to work and an objective philosophy of life. 'People who

put personal relationships before work become parasites on each
other, form mutual admiration societies . . .'[2] Spender writes in
secular terms, but his words may help in exegesis of the text
whether we apply it to our relations with Jesus or with other
people. We need a purpose and a loyalty beyond the humanly
personal. 'What is love between the sexes but an egoism for two?'
And friendship in which the element of carnal sexuality may not
enter at all into our consciousness or imagination, may nevertheless become the vehicle for our desire for power over other lives,
to possess and exploit them and suck them dry. Hence the devasta-
tions of jealousy. The truth was never more simply nor more
poignantly expressed than in the words of the soldier parting from
his mistress:

> I could not love thee, dear, so much,
> Loved I not honour more.

Human relations are validated and made perfect only by a loyalty
which transcends them.

It is the failure to understand this which places such great strain
on our human lives. For so many in our world faith in God has
gone. And we have tended to reverse the greater Johannine
affirmation and say, not 'God is love', but 'Love is God', which is
different and dangerous. Our human relations have been our chief
end and we have imposed such weight on them that they have
strained and broken. We have expected too much from friendship, too much from marriage, which though gifts beyond price,
find their fulfilment and meaning and their salvation only as they
are received from God and enjoyed in God. Our weak human
hearts may cling too much to these consolations, which though
worthy of all that we can give, and cause of inestimable joy, are but
frail human supports after all, the imperfect though real analogues
of the kingdom of heaven.

The Christian affirmation about Jesus, though its metaphysical
and poetic expressions may vary according to the fashions of
human thought, is what we have read so many times in our study
of the last discourses. Jesus is no longer with us as a human friend
because he has gone to God from whom he uniquely came. He has

ascended; and it is expedient for us that he has gone away. For him, too, his continuing work, his vocation towards God, is what matters supremely. He is not just 'Rabboni, my Master' as for Mary Magdalene, or even 'My Lord and My God' as for Thomas. He belongs to God and to the innumerable millions of the human race in every age – in Black Africa and China and Soviet Russia as much as in first-century Palestine or in a local church. And he is my Master and Lord because he is the everlasting Son of the Father and brings me into his own relation to God.

This is not the end of the Risen Lord's encounter with Mary Magdalene. 'Do not cling to me . . . Go to my brothers, *tell them* that I am ascending to my Father and your Father, to my God and your God.'

Some of the more radical theologians have been profoundly right when they have said that the ascended Christ is brought into our midst and made real by preaching. We are back here with the Johannine insistence on the word (see pp. 8f. above). It is essential to the proper relations of believers with their glorified Lord. It is to be widely interpreted. It involves meditation on the story as well as bare announcement; discussion and debate as well as pro-clamation. Mary Magdalene doubtless fulfilled Jesus's command excitedly, confusedly, incoherently – she would certainly have to answer questions about it and perhaps thereby come to frame convincing words of truth. If the appearances which follow in St John are supposed to be successive and not stories from the tradi-tion cobbled together, then Mary's first announcement did not bring the brothers immediately to assured faith. Preaching in whatever form, verbal communication, will often be half-heard, misunderstood, misapplied, lead to doubt as well as faith.

There is a time to keep silence as well as to speak. But in an age of incessant chatter when words pour from transistors and drown our thoughts, to speak and listen to God's word, his gospel, may rescue our human communications and set us free for those rela-tions which are fully enjoyed only in God. And the message of the Ascension was first entrusted to Mary Magdalene, the adoring, the devout, the sentimental, not only as an instance of God using the weak and those with strong emotions and the gift of tears, but to test and strengthen her faith by the discipline of the word whose servant she here becomes.

5. *The appearance to the ten.* John is vague about the place of the disciples' meeting, but the doors are shut, barred and bolted we may think. The disciples wish to conceal their whereabouts in case they share their Master's fate. Like the church in John's time and so many in our own, they dread the midnight knock of the secret police. And whatever evidence they have had of the resurrection, whatever Peter or the beloved disciple or Mary Magdalene have told them, has not given them the certainty which dispels fear. But the evangelist is more concerned to identify the first disciples with the situation of his own church than in narrative consistency.

The Risen Jesus cannot be kept out. He gives them the peace, a declaration not a wish, which became a liturgical greeting. The kiss of peace, or the passing of the peace, which had lapsed in many rites, has been revived in modern liturgies and, though contentious in some places and felt sometimes to be embarrassing to those who are strangers to the local fellowship, or even exclusive, it is deemed to fulfil the injunction of Matt. 5.23:

> If, when you are bringing your gift to the altar, you suddenly remember that your brother has a grievance against you, leave your gift where it is before the altar. First go and make peace with your brother, and only then come back and offer your gift.

The peace, in this sense, though its position in liturgies may vary, is always offered before communion, that people may not eat and drink unless they be 'in love and charity with their neighbours'. At St Giles Cathedral Edinburgh, in its fine liturgy, the peace is given as the communicants leave the circle which they have made around the Lord's Table after receiving the bread and wine. This is more the peace of the Easter Christ to his disciples. This follows the death and resurrection of the Lord and is the gift which he has bequeathed. 'Peace I leave with you. My peace I give unto you. Not as the world gives, give I unto you.' There should be room for two acts of peace in the eucharist – our reconciliation with one another and our welcome of strangers, and the peace of the Lord given when we have entered into his sacrifice; the assurance that we are one with him and that our troubled hearts, guilty because of our sin and fearful because of what may happen to us, are at rest.

And then Jesus shows his hands and his side, proof of his identity, and that he brings his whole life with him, risen from the dead. The disciples, filled with joy, receive again Christ's peace and his commission. 'As the Father sent me, so I send you.'

They are to be Christ's representatives on earth, their ministry continuous with his and with the same validity. It would not seem that John thinks of the ten as a special order within the church. They are nowhere called apostles in this book, even though they are sent. For John, discipleship is all, and he would agree with those in our time who regard this as 'the most fundamental concept of ecclesiology', even if he would have no truck with their jargon. There is no promotion out of discipleship.[3]

And the gift of the Holy Spirit – or Holy Spirit (there is no definite article in the Greek) – equips all disciples, with 'undistinguishing regard' and carries with it the power to remit and retain sins. 'Our Gospel presupposes an organized communal life, and with the absolution it also takes for granted the institution of an office through the risen Lord. However this office is not reserved for Peter, nor for the circle of apostles ... The disciples who receive commission, Spirit and authority from the risen Christ are simply the representatives of the Christian community.'

This is not to deny the legitimacy of ministerial priesthood on behalf of the priesthood of all believers. But every Christian has the right and often the duty to offer the divine forgiveness to the guilty and penitent. This is the great Christian privilege. The lay person may need to refer a penitent to one whose whole life has been devoted to a sacramental ministry of confession and absolution. But every disciple has the right to say to a desperate man or woman burdened with sin and looking to the Saviour, 'Your sins are forgiven, for Christ's sake.'

There is, however, the disturbing part: 'If you pronounce them unforgiven, unforgiven they remain.' It was true in the ministry of Jesus and it is true in the ministry of his disciples that some respond and some refuse. The former are forgiven; the latter may be hardened in their sin. This is a consequence of the preaching of the gospel; some see, some are made the more blind ... It is an awesome and terrible fact that there are those who will become worse because of the mission of Christ continued by his followers. 'If I had not come and spoken to them; they would not have sin; but now they have no excuse for their sin' (John 15.22). They are bound by it perhaps for ever.

6. *Thomas.* I interpret Thomas differently from the convention. He 'was not with them when Jesus came' and I think his absence is significant. Thomas was not a type of the scientific sceptic wanting visible, tangible proof. For one thing, I am not sure that so many scientists are like that. Some are quite credulous in things of religion; others of a theological inclination prefer Karl Barth, with his suspicion of natural theology, to Teilhard de Chardin, the Jesuit visionary with his biological optimism and creative evolution, beloved by Julian Huxley but not by all. It may be that it is not scientists but historians and students of literature who are likely to agonize in doubt, to cry out for evidence. Such doubt may be self-indulgent, like some devotions to the Passion, but the company of disciples needs those who 'know something of the depth and agony and the infinite burden of the cosmic wounds of Christ by which we are healed'.[4]

Thomas is a man of intense and somewhat withdrawn devotion, deliberately absent because the last thing he wants that evening is company, above all in a house church. He is in deep distress, ashamed of himself, totally in despair about his own salvation. He is not unlike Martin Luther in his monastic struggles, wondering if he could be saved, fearful that he might be as Augustine, his mentor, and Aquinas too, had warned him, predestined for damnation. In his intellectual and spiritual dark night Luther's confessor, von Staupitz told him: 'Leave such thoughts and begin with the wounds of Jesus.'

This is what Thomas would seek to do. He has heard rumours of Jesus come back from the dead. But for what? For judgment on him, not least. 'If only I could see the wounds.'

Hath he marks to lead me to him
If he be my guide?
In his feet and hands are wound prints
And his side.

Next week, on the eighth day, the day out of time and in the
kingdom, he is there. And Jesus shows him what he wants to see.
He believes and adores; acknowledges Christ's deity – 'My Lord
and my God' – but not as though he would say, 'I could recite the
Nicene Creed now, if the church had got that far.' If Thomas's
doubt was not that of the intellectual sceptic, his faith is not that
of intellectual conviction alone. It is believing, personal trust, total
adoring worship.

But no more than for the Magdalene is this faith and love all-
sufficient. The real beatitude is for those who know that Jesus has
gone to the Father, not to leave us desolate but that he may fill all
things. This transcends personal experience and confession.

There are perhaps more challenges to faith as time goes on and
the world grows in violence and, in spite of knowledge gained
and man come of age in the mastery of nature, injustice is rampant
and no human freedom safe. 'Where is the promise of his coming?'
we cry, and we may become superstitious and say 'Lo here! Lo
there!' and discern false Christs or become complacent about
nuclear warfare because we say this could be the expected end.
But though our faith be tested it is no more tried than that of the
disciples who saw the cross set up on Golgotha and went bewil-
dered to the tomb. Our beatitude, like theirs, is in Jesus returned to
God, conqueror even in his rejection by the world. Jesus, whom
we meet at his table and know, not only by the testimony of the
first disciples, but whose truth has been verified in saints and
martyrs and countless obscure and humble lives. Jesus, whose
praise has reached to the ends of the earth. Jesus, acknowledged in
the Te Deum, in the Creeds, in the Orthodox Liturgy, in the
Latin Mass, in the Book of Common Prayer and in the new forms
of our own day. Jesus, adored in the offices of monks and nuns
'when the yews were young that made the bows for Agincourt'
as now in the world of concrete jungles and shopping precincts.

Jesus, beloved of raucous Methodist field preachers, singing Wesley hymns and reading of eccentric Counter-Reformation pietists in *The Christian Library*; Jesus, served to the last in prison camps and by those who will not aquiesce in racial inequality or sell their souls for the false peace of the world. Jesus, the holy, meek, unspotted lamb, gentle and good, still bearing our sins, dumb and silent before his accusers, but the Christ also of Llandaff and Coventry, strong, majestic, our Judge; 'Christ of Revolution and of Poetry'; Jesus, the Crucified, risen from the dead, the same, yesterday, today and for ever, the Eternal Son, the way to the Father:

> That one Face far from vanish, rather grows
> Or decomposes but to recompose
> Become my Universe that feels and knows.

6 Post-Communion
John 21

The final chapter of St John's Gospel is generally regarded as an appendix, and one which spoils the artistic shape and balance of the work, even though there may be difficulties throughout which make us wonder if the author had quite 'got his act together' and would have re-written the whole had he had the chance, to refine the profound and original theology which the signs and sayings and stories adumbrate. Chapter 21 has a different style and quality from the discourses or the Passion. Yet to have been deprived of it, whoever wrote it, would be to have missed one of the most moving stories in the New Testament – the restoration of Peter – as well as to have lacked further insight into the meaning of discipleship. We shall treat it as giving guidance on the Christian life in the continuing world after worship is over – 'after breakfast' indeed, as verse 15 introduces the conversation with Peter; though we must begin at the beginning.

The disciples are still fishermen. And they are discouraged, even after the resurrection and the appearances, discouraged as the early Christians were in John's time, and as we are often now. Concerned to bring people in from the sea of the world to the kingdom, they toil in vain. They need the presence of the Risen Christ, apart from whom they can do nothing. None of the disciples in the Gospels catches any fish without Jesus.

He makes possible the perfect catch. The number 153 has allegorical meaning. The ancients believed that there were 153 kinds of fish in the sea and the Gospel is for all sorts and conditions, from every nation and kindred and people and tongue. The number is also of great interest to mathematicians, a triangular number which Hoskyns in his commentary illustrates with a diagram showing how 153 dots can be arranged in the form of an equilateral triangle with 17 dots on the base line. It is the perfect catch.

And the fact that the net is unbroken declares that the church's unity in the truth must not be broken in its mission to the world as so often it has been. Evangelism has been tragically divisive and evangelical Christians have sometimes been among the most quarrelsome. The unbroken net may also be a sign of that perfection in love which is the aim of evangelism. William Arthur, a very distinguished minister of the nineteenth century, said in the 1850s that Methodism had achieved much by conquest, little by nurture. The conquest – the miraculous haul – may not have been so evident since, but the test of mission is whether people really become one with Christ and grow in his grace.

The author cannot develop the simile of converts as fish too far, for evangelists cannot feed on those whom they convert, though some have tried to, by making them dependent, or even by reckoning their numbers to their own glory! In the second part of the chapter the fisherman Peter becomes the shepherd. His love for Christ must be revealed in his care for those who are Christ's. Pastors must always remember that the sheep, the people of God, are not theirs but Christ's. 'Feed *my* sheep.'

In the background is once more the mysterious alluring figure of the beloved disciple, who recognizes the Lord in the stranger on the shore and in his deep understanding represents those who, though they are able to discern Christ's living presence in the life, struggles and frustrations of his disciples are prepared to bear witness to him to the end, not perhaps by martyrdom but by the patience and the prayer that contends for the truth though his final coming be long delayed. Whatever the author of the Gospel believed about the eucharist, the beloved disciple is the archetype of sacramental Christianity which does not look for signs, other than those given in the word made flesh and feeds daily on him in the intimacy of the union he has made possible with the Father.

The last summons of the Risen Christ in St John is the same as the first of the Synoptic Gospels, 'Follow me!' There is only one vocation, that of discipleship, and everything else one does for Christ or his people derives from this.

It is important to follow. Christians often want to walk ahead of Christ, which leads to a discontent which is not divine, to that desire which Bonhoeffer castigated to have everything at once, 'matrimonial bliss, the cross, and the heavenly Jerusalem, where they neither marry nor are given in marriage'.[1] Sometimes we are so far behind that we lose sight of Christ altogether and there are depressing whispers that our voices have deceived us and that we should not have given Christ our hearts and that in any case we have no gifts for his service. Our self-doubt sometimes fostered by those who claim to be our candid friends should not deter us. We go on, following. And we may be encouraged by the wisdom of the Cappadocian Father of the fourth century, Gregory of Nyssa, who in his *Life of Moses* compares Moses, hidden in the cleft of the rock and allowed to see only God's back, with the following of Christ:

Now, he who follows sees the back.

So Moses, who eagerly seeks to behold God, is taught how he can behold him; to follow God wherever he might lead is to behold God. His passing by signifies his guiding the one who follows, for someone who does not know the way cannot complete his journey safely in any other way than by following behind his guide. He who leads then by his guidance shows the way to the one following. He who follows will not turn aside from the right way if he always keeps the back of his leader in view.

For he who moves to one side or brings himself to face his guide assumes another direction for himself than the one his guide shows him. Therefore he says to the one who is led, *My face is not to be seen*, that is 'Do not face your guide'. If he does so his course will certainly be in the opposite direction, for good does not look good in the face but follows it.[2]

This above all is true when we ask 'what will the end be?' We cannot be guaranteed evident success in our discipleship or the assurance that we shall be able at the last to trace a constant, over-ruling purpose.

The beloved disciple may have reached a serene old age, though not all who die peacefully in their beds are free from agony of spirit, or weariness 'in age and feebleness extreme'. And Browning's 'A Death in the Desert' pictures John in unclouded faith in the Christ of his Gospel, but escaping from persecutors, and from a church assailed by heretics and perverters of the truth.

Peter, on the other hand, will lose his freedom of movement and choice and die violently, a martyr, though the Lord's description of him could almost apply to someone in a wheel chair or a geriatric ward.

One never knows. God's judgment of a life cannot be determined by the manner of leaving it, else his own Son would be able to offer us no hope. Some of us would still want to use those 'words of such terrible weight'[3] at the committal in the Prayer Book Office for the Burial of the Dead: 'Suffer us not at our last hour for any pains of death to fall from thee.' But to this we would add the conclusion of a Methodist Bidding Prayer, which echoes ancient liturgies when it asks that God may 'direct the end of our lives to be Christian and well-pleasing in his sight, taking us to himself when he will and as he will, only without shame and sin'.

NOTES

Notes

Introduction

1. S. Paget, *Henry Scott Holland. Memoir and Letters*, 1921, p. 59; quoted in David Newsome, *Two Classes of Men*, John Murray 1974, p. 121.

2. For Irenaeus on *four* gospels see *Against Heresies* I, Ante Nicene Christian Library V, p. 287.

3. Donald MacKinnon, *Borderlands of Theology*, Lutterworth 1968, p. 92.

4. F. J. A. Hort, *The Way, The Truth, The Life*, Macmillan 1893, pp. 20f.

5. C. K. Barrett, *Essays on John*, SPCK 1982, p. 12.

6. See Hans-Josef Klauck, *Herrnmahl un hellenistischer Kult*, Aschendorff, Munster 1982.

7. G. Fox, *Journal* ed. N. Penney, Dent 1911, Vol I, p. 325.

8. Ernst Käsemann, *The Testament of Jesus*, SCM Press 1968, pp. 60, 61.

9. Aileen Guilding, *The Fourth Gospel and Jewish Worship*, OUP 1960. For the dialogue in St John see a fascinating paper by A. D. Nuttall in Michael Wadsworth (ed.), *Ways of Reading the Bible*, Harvester Press 1981, pp. 41ff. Nuttall applies some sophisticated methods of literary criticism to St John and concludes that the old, fierce alternative, 'either God or a wicked man', is posed for the unbelieving critic by the dialogues of Jesus. Or, he concludes that Jesus might have been mad, and yet spoken truth. It seems to me that he fails to convince because he regards the discourses as *ipsissima verba*.

1 The Preparation

1. Sir Edwyn Hoskyns, *The Fourth Gospel* ed. F. N. Davey, Faber and Faber 1947, pp. 443ff. For Never see *Allgemeine Deutsche Biographie*, XXIII, p. 564. I owe this information to Dr G. F. Nuttall.

2. This is probably more difficult than I have made it, as a conversation with Professor Evans after the chapter was written taught me. There seem to be two different interpretations joined together. 1. The foot-washing is the slave's act

and when paradoxically done by the Master it is to be copied by the disciple. This is a lesson in humility. 2. It is a sign, baptismal in character, and raises the question of cleansing and being cleansed. There is a similar problem in Mark 10.45 where the Son of Man is said to have come not to be ministered unto but to minister, but also to give his life a ransom for many. Does mutual foot-washing refer to the one or the other? Are the disciples humble servants or cleansers? In Phil. 2.5–11, the concept of Jesus as slave has become the vehicle of a doctrine of his person, and Christian service, the mutual forbearance of two women in the church, is dependent on the self-emptying of the Son of God. But humility and service are enjoined there, not cleansing, and this could be paramount in John 13.

3. J. H. Moulton, *A Neglected Sacrament*, Epworth Press 1919, p. 96.

4. Charles Péguy, *The Mystery of the Holy Innocents* tr. Pansy Pakenham, Harvill Press 1956.

5. J. H. Moulton, op. cit., p. 109.

6. A. E. Whitham, *The Discipline and Culture of the Spiritual Life*, Hodder and Stoughton 1938, pp. 40f.

7. E. Käsemann, op. cit., p. 38.

2 The Fencing of the Table

1. Cf. W. H. Cadman, *The Open Heaven*, Blackwell 1964, p. 137.

2. R. Bultmann, *The Gospel of John*, Blackwell 1971, p. 525.

3. Cf. Gabriel Marcel, *Being and Having*, Dacre Press 1949, p. 95 n. 1, where he quotes Antoine's remark in *Le Mort de Demain* that 'to love somebody is to say to him "You will not die" '.

3 The Ministry of the Word

1. Robert Seymour Bridges, *Noel: Christmas Eve 1913*.

2. Hort, op. cit., p. 32.

3. See Karl Rahner, 'Anonymous and Explicit Faith', *Theological Investigations* XVI, Darton, Longman and Todd 1975.

4. W. F. Howard, *Christianity According to St John*, Duckworth 1943, p. 182. Cf. R. C. Zaehner's inaugural lecture, *Foolishness to the Greeks*, OUP 1953.

5. R. Bultmann, op. cit., pp. 379–80.

6. K. Barth, *Epistle to the Romans* tr. E. C. Hoskyns, OUP 1933, p. 258.

7. R. Bultmann, op. cit., pp. 606–7.

8. Hort, op. cit., p. 35.

9. The phrase 'His absence is as his presence' has an echo of R. S. Thomas's poem 'Sea-Watching', *Laboratories of the Spirit*, Macmillan 1975.

10. For Congar and Ignatius see Andrew Louth, *Discerning the Mystery*, Clarendon Press 1983, p. 93.

11. W. H. Cadman, op. cit., p. 160.

12. This phrase is from Henry Scott Holland, quoted by Donald MacKinnon, 'Scott Holland and Contemporary Needs', *Borderlands of Theology*, Lutterworth Press 1968, p. 115; also by C. F. Evans, *Resurrection and the New Testament*, SCM Press 1970, p. 142, both without reference.

13. For the Puritans see Walter Marshall, *The Gospel Mystery of Sanctification*, London 1692; also my *Puritan Devotion*, Epworth Press 1957.

14. Charles Smyth, *The Friendship of Christ*, Longmans, Green and Co. 1945, pp. 38f. Reprinted by permission of Hodder and Stoughton Ltd.

15. E. C. Hoskyns and Noel Davey, *Crucifixion-Resurrection*, SPCK 1981, p. 145.

4 The Prayer of 'Consecration'

1. E. C. Hoskyns, *The Fourth Gospel*, pp. 494f.

2. The translation of the *Didache* is taken from R. C. D. Jasper and G. J. Cuming (ed.), *Prayers of the Eucharist*, Collins 1979, p. 1.

3. Dietrich Bonhoeffer, *Letters and Papers from Prison*, The Enlarged Edition, SCM Press 1971, p. 199.

4. See D. Z. Phillips, *The Concept of Prayer*, Blackwell ²1982, pp. 115–17.

5. E. C. Hoskyns, *We are the Pharisees*, SPCK 1961, pp. 63, 64.

6. John Burnaby, *Amor Dei*, Hodder and Stoughton 1938, p. 18.

Throughout this chapter I am much indebted to Christopher Evans' lecture, 'Christ at Prayer in St John's Gospel' from *Lumen Vitae* XXIV, 4 (International Studies in Religious Education, Brussels). I do not accept his argument that *hagiazein* should be given its meaning of separate from the profane with no sacrificial connotation, but I have drawn freely on much of his exposition.

5 Crucifixion – Resurrection – Communion

1. The quotation from Paul Tillich is from the sermon 'Born in a Grave' in *The Shaking of the Foundations*, SCM Press 1949. The argument here is much indebted to writings of Professor Donald MacKinnon, especially in *The Problem of Metaphysics*, CUP 1974, pp. 119f.

2. Stephen Spender, *The Thirties and After*, Fontana 1978, pp. 114ff.

3. E. Käsemann, op. cit., p. 29. Robert Murray, 'The Features of Early Christian Asceticism', Peter Brooks (ed.), *Christian Spirituality*, SCM Press 1975, p. 69.

Concerning attraction to Jesus, as in Mary Magdalene's desire to touch him in the Easter Garden, I would call attention to a profound discussion in Donald MacKinnon's Gifford Lectures *The Problem of Metaphysics*, also referred to above. It is in the chapter on 'The Notion of Presence' (p. 152), and cites a passage in Kant's *Tugendlehre*, in which, when Kant talks of love, 'he insists that when two human beings love each other there must obtain in their relationship something analogous to gravitation, the complementary operation of attractive and repulsive force. One human being may be drawn to another (and Kant is clearly thinking both of sexual love and of friendship); there is an obvious attraction between them. Indeed, in speaking of them of being drawn to each other, one is already using this idiom. But out of this attraction may come two consequences, both alike damaging. One person may seek to dominate the other, to impose upon the other his views of the world, indeed of their relationship. Alternatively, one person may become infatuated with the one he believes himself to love so that the other (it may be unintentionally) becomes the occasion of a sort of infatuation as destructive of authentic relationship as the kind of egoistic domination mentioned a moment ago. In both cases the outcome is destructive. It is Kant's view that such domination can only be avoided when a proper respect enables each of the two to hold the other at a certain distance, seeking neither to dominate nor to yield to a sort of slavish subordination. Here there is in Kant's view a complementarity analogous to that supplied in gravity by the repulsion which balances attraction.' Reprinted by permission of the Cambridge University Press.

4. Daniel T. Jenkins, *The Gift of Ministry*, Faber 1947, p. 63.

6 Post-Communion

1. Bonhoeffer, *Letters and Papers from Prison*, p. 169.

2. Gregory of Nyssa, *The Life of Moses* (*Classics of Western Spirituality*), Paulist Press and SPCK 1979, pp. 119–20.

3. Iris Murdoch, *An Unofficial Rose*, Penguin 1964, p. 14. For contrasted views as to their Christian validity see John Barnaby on 'Christian Prayer' in A. R. Vidler (ed.), *Soundings*, CUP 1962, p. 236, and John Bowker, 'The Human Imagination of Hell', *Theology*, November 1982, p. 410.